Gainesville

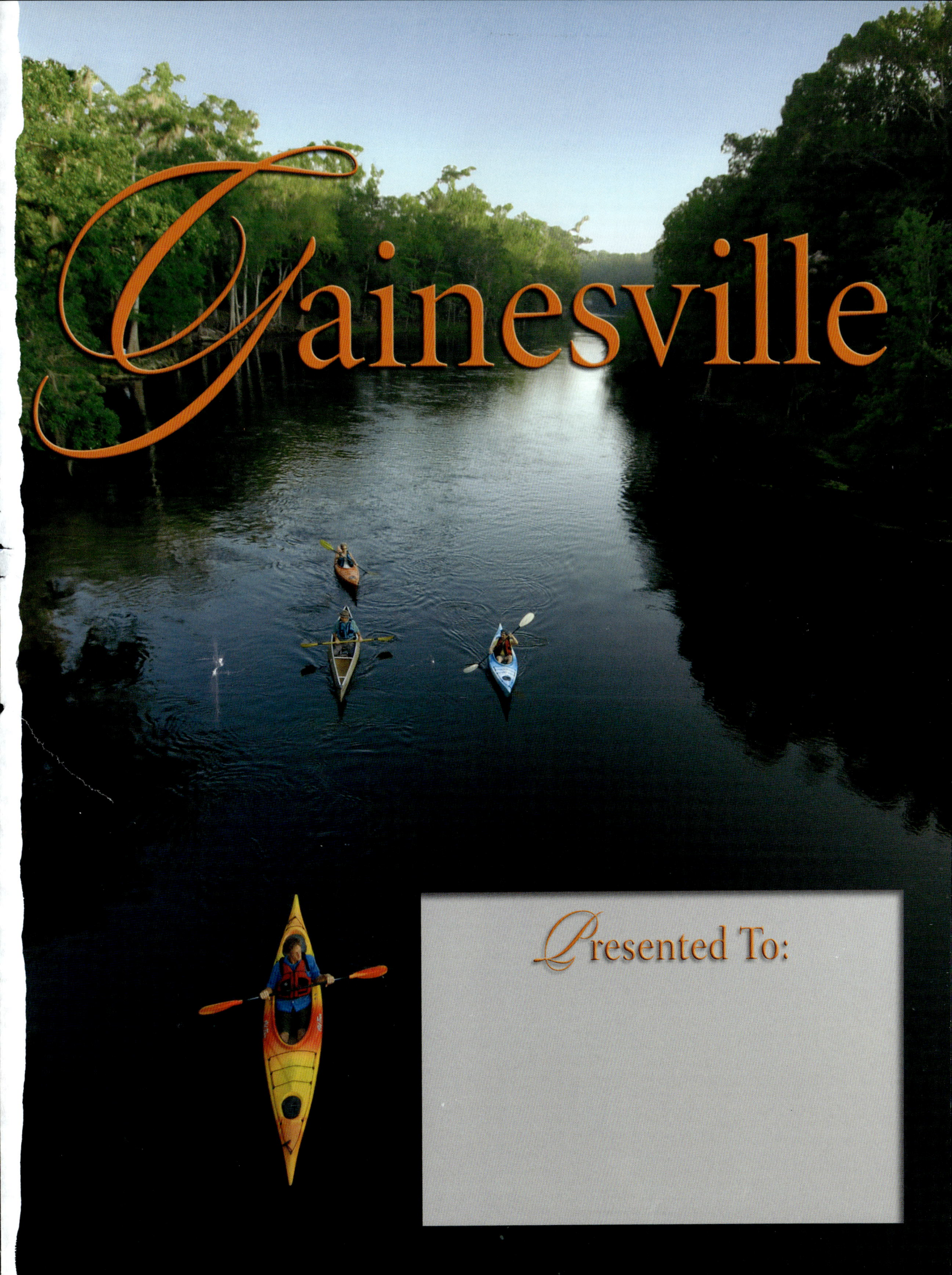

Presented To:

PHOTO BY GENE BEDNAREK

The Swamp, as the Ben Hill Griffin Stadium at Florida Field is affectionately named, has undergone many additions throughout its history and now holds more than ninety thousand fans. In fact, it seems like every home game is a big game, and every big game has "a record crowd." Even though it doesn't take much to get that many fanatics fired up, the Gator cheerleaders start the pregame activities with the famous "Orange and Blue" chant, pitting the alumni side against the student side to see which can shout their color the loudest.

Gainesville

RIVERBEND BOOKS
A division of BOOKHOUSE GROUP, INC.

EVERY PATH *starts with* PASSION

Gainesville
Every Path *starts with* Passion

EDITOR	Rob Levin
PUBLISHER	Barry Levin
ASSOCIATE PUBLISHER	Bob Sadoski
COMMUNITY LIAISON	Sonia Douglas
CHIEF OPERATING OFFICER	Renée Peyton
ASSOCIATE EDITOR	Rena Distasio
PROJECT DIRECTOR	Cheryl Sadler
PHOTO EDITOR	Jill Dible
WRITERS	Kimberly DeMeza, Rena Distasio, Grace Hawthorne, Amy Meadows, Regina Roths, Gail Snyder
COPY EDITOR	Bob Land
BOOK DESIGN	Compòz Design
JACKET DESIGN	Kevin Smith
PREPRESS	Vickie Berdanis
PHOTOGRAPHERS	Gene Bednarek, Douglas Henderson, Scott Indermaur, Matt Marriott, Dom Martino, Rod Reilly, Alan S. Weiner

Copyright © 2008 by Bookhouse Group, Inc.
Printed and bound in Korea
All rights reserved. No part of this book may be reproduced or transmitted in any form or by any means, electronic or mechanical, including photocopying of records, or by any information storage and retrieval system without permission in writing from Bookhouse Group, Inc.

Published by Riverbend Books
an Imprint of Bookhouse Group, Inc.
818 Marietta Street, NW
Atlanta, Georgia 30318
www.riverbendbooks.net
404.885.9515

Gainesville : every path starts with passion.
    p. cm.
Edited by Rob Levin.
ISBN 978-1-883987-35-0
 1. Gainesville (Fla.)—Pictorial works. 2. Gainesville (Fla.)—Social life and customs—Pictorial works. I. Levin, Rob, 1955-
F294.G16G35 2008
975.9'79—dc22
            2008012541

PHOTO BY DOUG HENDERSON

With both coasts only ninety minutes away and less than an hour's drive to the St. John's River, great fishing in the Gainesville region is not only easy, but inevitable. However, this city's residents don't have to travel to enjoy one of their favorite sports, because they can cast their lines in six nearby freshwater lakes. Undoubtedly, such ample angling opportunities influenced *Sperling's Best Places* to list Gainesville as a Top Ten City in the USA for Outdoor Activities. Here, fourteen-year-old Brinson Harris appears to be on top of the world as he awaits a bite from one of Orange Lake's delectable bass.

GAINESVILLE — EVERY PATH *starts with* PASSION

PHOTO BY SCOTT INDERMAUR

PHOTO BY DOUG HENDERSON

Foreword 11

16

Your journey of discovery begins here, as words and images unfold to reveal Gainesville's unique story.

Featured Companies 192

Learn about the companies, organizations, and individuals whose spirit infuses this book—and makes Gainesville such a wonderful place to be.

8 GAINESVILLE — EVERY PATH *starts with* PASSION

Contents

PHOTO BY GENE BEDNAREK

PHOTO BY MATT MARRIOTT

About the Publisher 198

Every day is a day of discovery for the team dedicated to crafting some of this country's finest and award-winning pictorial books.

Editorial Team 199

The storytellers behind the storybooks, Riverbend's acclaimed photographers and writers delight in capturing the essence of our nation's communities.

GAINESVILLE — EVERY PATH *starts with* PASSION 9

PHOTO BY ALAN S. WEINER

Little Chloe Crosby enjoys a bird's-eye view of the Hoggetowne Medieval Faire from atop her father Timothy's shoulders. Family-style events like this one abound in Gainesville, providing moms and dads with plenty of creative answers to the question: "What do you want to do this weekend?"

10 GAINESVILLE — EVERY PATH *starts with* PASSION

Foreword

Gainesville has come a long way since its founding in 1854 with a population of only 250. Today, our community offers something for everyone. Theatre, museums, sporting events, the charm of historic districts, and the beauty of Florida wildlife and nature are just a few of the many elements that make Gainesville a wonderful place to live. But Gainesville is also a wonderful economic environment for new local businesses, ranking No. 12 in the April edition of *Forbes* magazine for the best places to do business and have a career, and listed in the 100 Best Places to Live and Launch by *Fortune Small Business* magazine.

Gainesville is home to the prestigious University of Florida, Florida's oldest public university, and the nationally renowned Santa Fe Community College, both institutions attracting thousands of top students and faculty from all around the world and bringing energy and excitement to our community. As a center of innovations in science and medicine, Shands Hospital at UF and North Florida Regional Medical Center bring the best and brightest in the medical field to Gainesville.

Gainesville has also surfaced as a thriving active adult community. Recently, the city was ranked eighth among the Top Ten Value Towns for Those Considering Retirement in 2007, and was No. 11 on an AARP list of Best Places to Reinvent Your Life.

In 2007 alone, Gainesville was ranked No. 1 in Frommer's Cities Ranked, No. 3 on NuWire Investor's list of the Top 10 Small College Towns for Investment, and one of the 50 Best Places to Live and Play according to *National Geographic Adventure* magazine. Additionally, Gainesville welcomed three NCAA championship teams from the University of Florida during the 2006 and 2007 seasons.

The national recognition has only served to reinforce what those in our community already know: Gainesville is an amazing place to live, work, and play. Enjoy this portrait of life in a place where "every path starts with passion."

Brent Christensen
President and Chief Executive Officer

PHOTO BY DOUG HENDERSON

12 GAINESVILLE — Every Path *starts with* Passion

When the lights come on just outside of the Hippodrome State Theatre, the stunning architecture of the historic Federal Building is on display. The structure, built circa 1909, is one of the city's most elegant examples of Palladium Classical Revival architecture, making it a natural centerpiece for the downtown area. The six Corinthian limestone columns at the entrance of the building are evidence of the dazzling experience that awaits visitors once they get inside. And when they do walk through the elaborately designed bronze entry doors and across the polished terrazzo floors, it's like they've stepped into another world. That feeling is reinforced when they are treated to some of the finest theatre the Gainesville arts community has to offer. It's the type of adventure this gentleman looks forward to as he takes a few moments to admire the property from an absolutely perfect vantage point.

Gainesville

EVERY PATH *starts with* PASSION

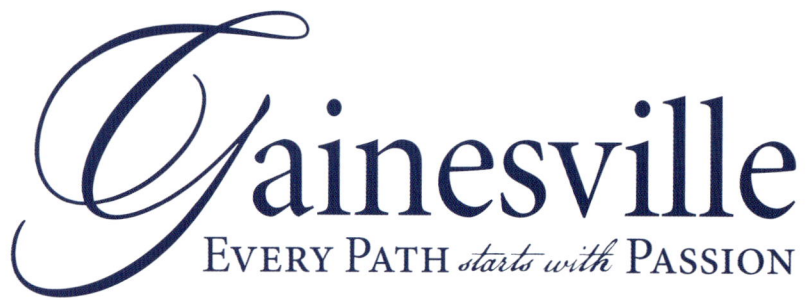

would not have been possible without the support of the following sponsors:

Alachua County Biotech Industry | Best Western Gateway Grand | Bosshardt Realty Services Inc. | Brice Development Inc. | Crime Prevention Security Systems and Custom Home Entertainment | Fletcher Mortgage Company | Florida Citizens Bank | Gainesville Harley-Davidson & Buell | Gainesville Health & Fitness Center | M.M. Parrish Construction Company | Santa Fe Community College | Santa Fe HealthCare Inc. / AvMed Health Plans | Tioga Realty | Tioga Town Center | Town of Tioga

Alachua County Biotech Industry

BIOFLORIDA

UF | Sid Martin Biotechnology Incubator
UNIVERSITY of FLORIDA

RTI | BIOLOGICS™

A G T C

BOSSHARDT
REALTY SERVICES INC

NOVAMIN TECHNOLOGY, INC.

Best Western

brytan

FLETCHER
MORTGAGE COMPANY

FLORIDA CITIZENS BANK
YOUR 7 TO 7 BANK

Gainesville
MOTOR HARLEY-DAVIDSON CYCLES
Buell
Harley-Davidson & Buell

GAINESVILLE
Health&Fitness
CENTER

MM Parrish
CONSTRUCTION CO.

SANTA FE COMMUNITY COLLEGE
ALACHUA & BRADFORD COUNTIES
EST. 1966

AvMed
HEALTH PLANS

TIOGA REALTY
Residential & Commercial Services

TIOGA TOWN CENTER

TOWN of TIOGA
What life should feel like.

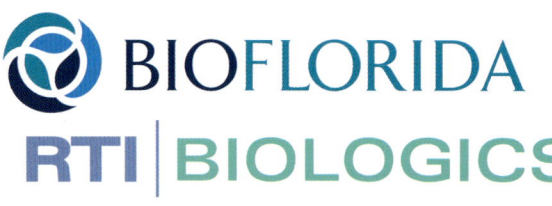

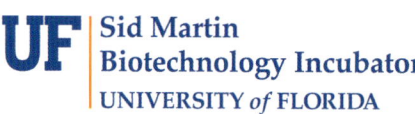

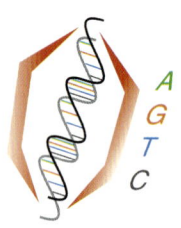

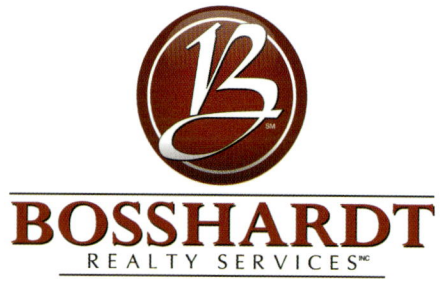

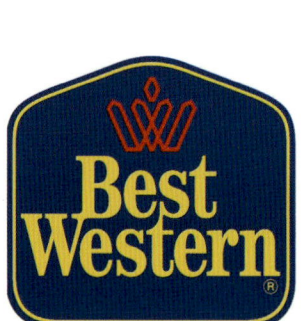

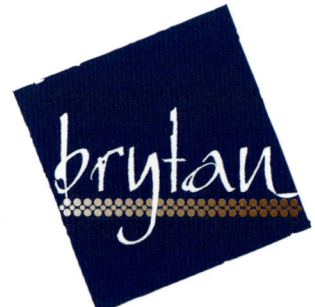

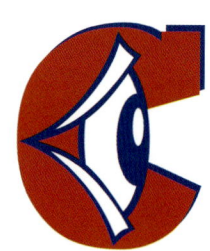

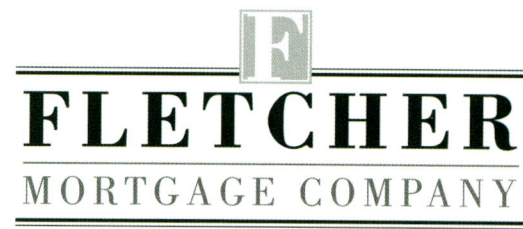

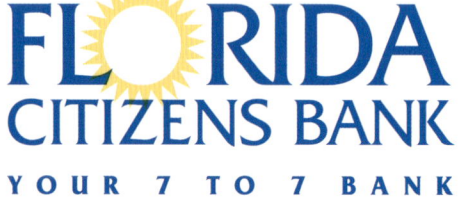

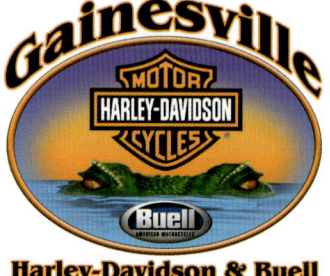

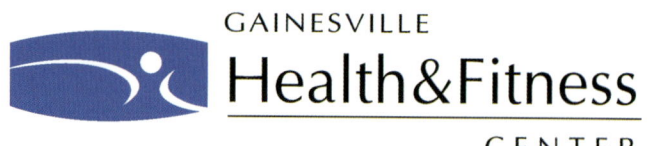

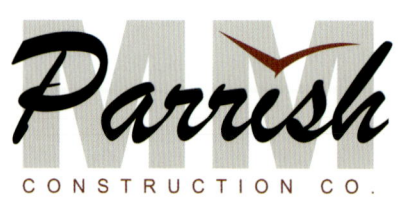

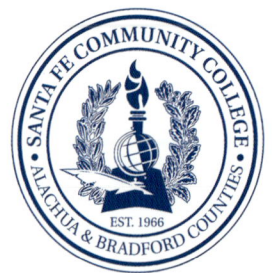

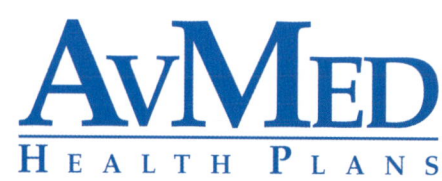

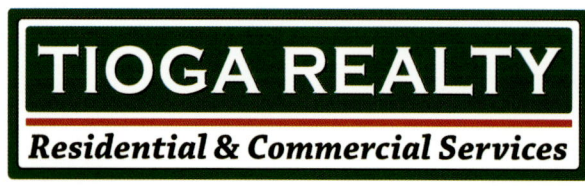

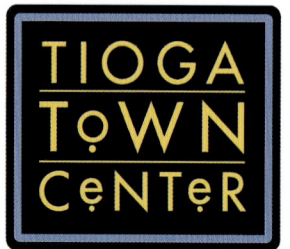

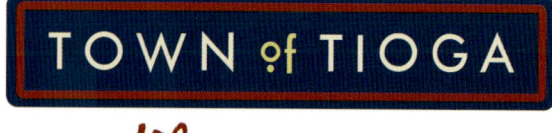

One of the most recognizable Gainesville landmarks is the regal Clock Tower that stands on E. University Avenue. Sitting atop the tower, which was designed in the style of the city's original 1885 courthouse, is the actual clock that once kept time in that building. When the courthouse was demolished, the clock was painstakingly removed. In 1983, the impressive timepiece was installed in the new clock tower. To this day, it continues to mark the minutes of the day for the people who call the city home.

ALL PHOTOS BY GENE BEDNAREK

M
ost people associate Florida with outstanding beaches, but the waterways of North Florida offer a unique kind of beauty not to be missed. The area is blessed with cypress swamps, hardwood swamps, river hardwood forests, darkwater rivers, spring runs, and marshes, each with specific secrets to explore. Adventure Outpost Tours leads canoe and kayak trips on more than forty waterways, including manatee viewing tours. Local guides with a lifetime of experience take pride in sharing their state's wonders and the legacy of prehistoric inhabitants, human history, and natural beauty that the wetlands offer.

16 GAINESVILLE — E VERY P ATH *starts with* P ASSION

PHOTO BY DOUG HENDERSON

It's almost hard to believe that a bustling city like Gainesville is only moments away from a setting of such unparalleled repose. But that's what makes Alachua County so special. It offers an amazing blend of metropolitan excitement while affording residents and visitors the chance to get away from it all and truly commune with nature any time they please. Lush backdrops, complete with breathtaking sunsets, juxtapose seamlessly with the liveliness of a flourishing city, where culture and a sense of joviality are apparent day and night. And as each day ends, there is always the promise of something even more invigorating for the next twenty-four hours, whether it's within the city limits or out in the natural world that waits beyond its borders.

GAINESVILLE — EVERY PATH *starts with* PASSION 17

Tioga Town Center Mixes It Up

When developers Miguel and Luis Diaz created their vision for Town of Tioga, they took a bold step into the future by embracing design concepts from the past. The master-planned community they conceived would be modeled after pre–World War II building patterns—a neighborhood in which residents would have a communal place to stroll along pedestrian-friendly streets, shop for daily necessities, unwind after a long day, gather for special events, and even call home. In 2003, that image really began to take shape when ground was broken for Tioga Town Center, a modern-day, mixed-use development in the heart of town that would bring together residential, retail, and commercial resources and serve as the center of life for this burgeoning suburb.

According to Grace Lambert, director of marketing and leasing, Tioga Town Center "was intended to be the jewel at the gateway to a traditional community, but purposefully located to be easily accessible to the entire surrounding community." That goal has been achieved, as the initial eighty-three-thousand-square-foot phase of the center, comprising retail, office, and health and fitness space, has become one of the most popular commercial and retail developments in the Gainesville area. One reason for the popularity is the fact that establishments that have located in the center represent a mix of nationally recognized businesses that provide familiarity and credibility to the shopping experience and local businesses that reflect "what is unique to our beautiful community and truly give it its own flavor," says Lambert.

In addition, Tioga Town Center is the site for numerous charitable events, interactive festivals that highlight local artisans, and one

> Tioga Town Center was intended to be the jewel at the gateway to a traditional community.

Many of the retail stores in Tioga Town Center offer more than just an excellent shopping opportunity. In fact, shops like the Cucina Mia Gourmet Kitchen Store have turned themselves into bona fide destinations by offering a variety of classes and workshops. Here Karen Chiappone conducts a food and wine pairing class for customers who are eager to expand their culinary horizons.

PHOTO BY ROD REILLY

PHOTO BY ROD REILLY

of the area's largest farmers markets. The combination, she adds, "invites participation from all walks of the community." In fact, the presence of Tioga Town Center in the Gainesville area, which is typically known for its large student population, is attractive to the educated professionals, young families, and retirees who are now migrating to the area. Lambert continues, "Tioga Town Center has developed at a time when there has been a void in fulfilling many of the services and retail choices desired by these particular demographic groups."

What's more, with its residential offerings, including the second- and third-story apartments that are part of the ninety-thousand-square-foot phase that broke ground in November 2007, Tioga Town Center has managed to give the development a distinctive urban flair as well. This unique characteristic makes the area an ideal living environment—as well providing as an outstanding quality of life—for residents of all ages, who will be able to enjoy the community's blend of environmentally friendly design, architectural

Continued on page 20

When the sun goes down, there's still much to do in Tioga Town Center. For exercise enthusiasts, the Gainesville Health and Fitness Center is a great place to get in an evening workout. The fully equipped twenty-four-hour facility welcomes individuals of all experience levels with its state-of-the-art workout equipment and more than nine hundred group fitness classes each month.

Tioga Town Center

PHOTO BY ROD REILLY

The smell of warm bread just out of the oven will make anyone feel right at home. That's why the Flour Pot Bakery has been the perfect addition for Tioga Town Center; everyone who walks by the charming shop and catches a whiff of its enticing goods gets the sense of being close to home.

PHOTO BY GENE BEDNAREK

Tioga Town Center continued from page 19

detail, considerable convenience, and Smart Growth principles for years to come.

"Our goal for the Tioga Town Center is to create a synergistic place that the community makes part of its everyday life—whether for living or work or pleasure, we want the town center to represent a heart at the center of the area's most significant growth," Lambert explains. "Every person who moves here becomes a part of Gainesville, a community we love. We want Tioga Town Center to be a part of what is best in our town."

There's nothing like getting up in the morning and heading down to the local coffee shop for that much-needed jolt of caffeine. Fortunately for the residents of Tioga, one of the finest coffee suppliers is right around the corner. Conveniently located in Tioga Town Center, Starbucks makes it easy to get a coffee fix any time of the day.

20 GAINESVILLE — EVERY PATH *starts with* PASSION

Life in the Town of Tioga certainly is sweet, and it's made even sweeter by the presence of Peterbrooke Chocolatier in Tioga Town Center. This delightful shop offers a wide selection of delectable confections, from truffles to chocolate-covered strawberries, affording residents and visitors of all ages a convenient way to satisfy their sweet tooth.

PHOTO BY ROD REILLY

Various organizations have applauded that effort. In addition to recognition from the National Association of Home Builders for Best in Living Smart Growth Communities, Tioga Town Center received an award from the city of Gainesville for Outstanding Contribution to City Beautification. The development has earned these accolades for its attention to detail in preserving green space, for using resources wisely, and for considering the impact these endeavors will have on the future—all of which will be applied to every element of the center, which will total approximately three hundred thousand square feet upon completion. As Lambert concludes, "Our goal is to create a gathering place for the community—a place for daily commerce and a place that represents the family-oriented lifestyle of Americans today." ∎

PHOTO BY ROD REILLY

R&R is the name of the game in Tioga. After a leisurely weekend stroll through Tioga Town Center, locals can head home with the soothing products they purchased at the Bath Junkie for a peaceful bubble bath or a refreshing manicure or pedicure. And they can indulge in that kind of leisure any time they please, thanks to the store's great location in the heart of the community.

GAINESVILLE — EVERY PATH *starts with* PASSION   21

"Movement and Life" is the invigorating creed for the Dance Alive National Ballet, headquartered in Gainesville and named the State Touring Company of Florida for thirty-two consecutive years. Blending artistry, elegance, and when appropriate, comedic flair, this company's international roster includes acclaimed dancers from the United States, Russia, China, Brazil, Japan, Uruguay, Chile, and Cuba. The company is also proud of its successful children's troupe: Ladybug Action Hero. These Arts Ambassadors for the City of Gainesville, led by Kim Tuttle, artistic director, and Judy Skinner, choreographer-in-residence, tour the southeastern United States and Costa Rica with repertoire and classics such as *The Nutcracker*. "We usually don't tour with the *Cleopatra* performance because it's a really big ballet," states Tuttle, explaining that Michele Incollingo, pictured here as the Egyptian queen with Noodle, an albino Burmese python, doesn't mind sharing her dressing room with the theatrical reptile. She's also grateful that Noodle isn't an asp.

ALL PHOTOS BY SCOTT INDERMAUR

GAINESVILLE — EVERY PATH *starts with* PASSION 23

Boo-At-The-Zoo draws more than six thousand visitors each Halloween to the Santa Fe Community College Teaching Zoo. Costumed zookeepers give out more than ninety-two thousand pieces of candy, and the canned goods collected as the cost of admission are donated to area food banks.

Brytan: A Community Representing the Best of Today with the Charm of Yesterday

In the "good old days," neighbors greeted one another as they passed on the sidewalks and kids played in the park before riding their bikes to the local drugstore for a soda. Neighborhood and town were closely integrated.

People often long for those communities of yesteryear, but think that those communities don't exist anymore. Think again! Brice Group, a family-owned business, has envisioned Brytan—"the unexpected neighborhood." The company, formed more than seventy years ago by Carl and Hazel Brice, is building the type of community that features the best of the past, but they're accessorizing it with today's conveniences and technology.

> A mixed-use development, Brytan offers a lifestyle that doesn't require an automobile to go everywhere.

Every home in Brytan is required to meet a level of green building certification through EnergyStar, Florida Green Building Coalition, or the Leadership in Energy & Environmental Design (LEED) standard. A commitment to environmentally sustainable design is evident throughout Brytan, as is a commitment to quality craftsmanship. Builders in Brytan must belong to the Brytan Guild, a group of tradespeople rated by their customers to provide quality building and high customer service.

A mixed-use development, Brytan offers a lifestyle that doesn't require an automobile to go everywhere. The neighborhood is designed to meet the daily needs of residents and welcomes visitors. Andres Duany, renowned land planner and architect, led a design team to master plan the community. The result is a variety of housing options—from townhouses to bungalows, from rental

Continued on page 26

Brytan's many beautiful parks and green spaces make ideal spots for almost any outdoor activity.

GAINESVILLE — EVERY PATH *starts with* PASSION 25

Brice Development Inc.

PHOTO BY DOUG HENDERSON

Brice Development continued from page 25

apartments to live/work units—carefully mixed with retail stores, boutiques, dining choices, and recreation opportunities. The Brytan plan encompasses approximately 150 acres, including parks, walking trails, and gardens. The Town Center, centered along Market Street, will offer unique dining and shopping experiences for the residents living in the community and tenants occupying the commercial spaces now available for lease or purchase.

For those who aren't employed within Brytan's boundaries, several employers are so nearby that the words " long commute" become obsolete. The University of Florida, Nationwide Insurance, Shands Hospital, and the Cancer Center are all within an easy drive or bus ride. "We're anticipating that we will attract doctors, nurses, and technicians who want to be close to the hospital," explains Sara Summerfield, marketing director.

The Brytan community embraces the best of the old—a close-knit neighborhood feel—with the best of the new—commercial space and fiber optic network throughout. The lifestyle offered includes short to no commutes to work, walk-to restaurants and entertainment, and green getaways.

The Brytan Conceptual Master Development Plan represents 150 acres of a mixed-use development dubbed "the unexpected neighborhood" by the Brice Group. Residents will have full access to parks, walking trails, and gardens conveniently located near a variety of living spaces ranging from bungalows to single-family homes. Brytan is located at the intersection of Archer Road and Tower Road.

Brytan offers another attraction for business owners and residents—Brytlink—a fiber optic network wired into every home and available to every business. This system provides high bandwidth and a secure connection for transferring information. "Not only are we close to the hospitals, but if someone has a second office or home office in Brytan it will be a secure connection for them to send information to and from the hospital," Summerfield says.

Ultimately, Brytan combines the best of the past with the accommodations of the future. As its founders like to say, "No matter where you are in life—Brytan is for you." ■

Make commutes a thing of the past. With offices, boutiques, and markets in the neighborhood, you can get to work, shopping, and dining without having to hop in the car. Plus, Brytan offers Brytlink—a fiber optic network wired into all living spaces and available to the development's business owners.

GAINESVILLE — EVERY PATH *starts with* PASSION   27

With its spacious lawns, rose-lined walkways, jasmine-draped gazebo, and ancient oaks dripping with moss, the Herlong Mansion is the perfect place for an intimate, elegant wedding. The grounds and grand front porch provide a memorable setting for outdoor occasions, while indoor events take place in the property's antique bedecked banquet hall. Add a white dove release and a departure by horse and carriage, and you have a once-in-a-lifetime ceremony, never to be forgotten.

ALL PHOTOS BY DOUG HENDERSON

When the Haile family moved from South Carolina to Gainesville in 1856, their homestead became a fondly remembered gathering place for the community. Today it remains as the inspiration for a neighborhood designed to bring back the Victorian ambience and small-town comfort of days gone by combined with the conveniences of modern life—Haile Plantation. The Haile Village Center Meeting Hall at the hub of the development overlooks oak- and flower-lined walkways leading to the central fountain of the Village Green. Main Street's shops, restaurants, and businesses make life a breeze for residents who can work so nearby that they have time to walk home for lunch. The award-winning plan includes a golf course, bike and walking trails, swimming, tennis, and a country club—all in a traditional setting that provides a heavenly lifestyle for anyone fortunate enough to occupy one of Haile Plantation's twenty-seven hundred custom homes, townhouses, apartments, or condominiums.

GAINESVILLE — EVERY PATH *starts with* PASSION

Clariant Life Science Molecules (FL) Inc.

Clariant Life Science Molecules: Exactly Your Chemistry

Chemistry is such an integral part of our lives that it would be hard to imagine the world without it. Chemical substances help provide comfort, write history, change habits, and transform visions and ideas into the reality of finished products. This last point best describes what Clariant does at its facility in Gainesville.

"We make specialty intermediate chemicals, primarily adaptations of the silicone molecule," says Brian Soucek, human resources manager. "Our products go into the manufacture of many high-tech items such as pharmaceuticals, personal care products, semiconductor chips, contact lenses, and automotive coatings. Working with our customers we can understand their technical applications and improve either the end-user product or a component of the manufacturing process. We help make our customer's product more durable, more resilient, easier to make, or more environmentally friendly to produce."

Such high-tech solutions require specialized development by the Clariant Gainesville site's team of dedicated employees. Says Soucek, "Business development and marketing specialists, scientists, chemical engineers, production engineers, production operators, maintenance mechanics, lab technicians, and administrative specialists all contribute to meeting our customers' needs."

"It takes a determined and coordinated effort, but we are committed to doing it right and following the guidelines set by federal, state, and county agencies," says site director Helen Miyasaki.

Attention to detail has been a cornerstone at the Gainesville facility since University of Florida professors Dr. Paul Tarrant and the

> **C**hemical substances help provide comfort, write history, change habits, and transform visions and ideas into the reality of finished products.

Justin Kendrick, operations technician, monitors the continuous processing of silicone intermediates.

PHOTO BY ROD REILLY

30 GAINESVILLE — EVERY PATH *starts with* PASSION

late Dr. George Butler founded the original firm in 1953. Today Clariant is a global leader in the field of specialty chemicals.

"Of all the Clariant sites, we consider Gainesville the best place to work, live, and raise a family," Miyasaki says. "We cultivate a family atmosphere here and provide excellent benefits for our employees. We also believe it is equally important to be a good corporate citizen."

To that end, Clariant is a primary sponsor for the Cystic Fibrosis Foundation Walk each spring. "We became aware of this opportunity when one of our employee's children was diagnosed with cystic fibrosis in 2000," says Miyasaki. "A coworker spearheaded the drive in this area, and we have continued our support."

Clariant also supports the development of math and science education in the community by donating time and money for local and regional science fairs; partnering with Howard Bishop Middle School, the local science and technology magnet school; and sponsoring the Alachua County Science Teacher of the Year award.

Like the products they produce, it would be hard to imagine Gainesville without the involvement of Clariant and its employees. ■

Dr. Michael Wilson, R&D senior scientist, tests a mixture of silicone emulsifiers for a personal care application.

ALL PHOTOS BY SCOTT INDERMAUR

There must be thousands of pizza joints in Florida, but this one has a *philosophy*. It's Satchel's Pizza and Satchel's philosophy, and it goes something like this: "People always say that a restaurant is 'location, location, location,' but I never believed that.... If you make good food and serve it in a comfortable setting, people will come." And they do because Satchel's has the funkiest décor and best pizza in Gainesville. Or maybe it's the fact that like Taylor Wilson, Ginger Stima, and Bryan Flood, you can get your pizza served to you in the blue VW bus that sits out front. Satchel's Pizza is not fast food: "If you're in a hurry you may just want a slice. Enjoy some live music from Travis Whitton and his band, relax, and we'll make it worth the wait." That's profound.

PHOTO BY GENE BEDNAREK

Santa Fe Community College's Kika Silva Pla Planetarium boasts two of the finest digital star projectors in the world. The planetarium offers public shows every weekend and is your guide to the night sky over North Central Florida.

Bosshardt Realty Services, Inc.

Bosshardt Realty: Family Owned and Leading Edge

Carol Bosshardt, president and CEO of Bosshardt Realty Services, Inc., likes to be challenged. Give her five reasons that something will not work, and she will give you ten reasons why it will. Twenty years ago, despite the odds, she firmly believed she could take on the national real estate chains and not only survive, but succeed. And succeed she has.

Today, Bosshardt Realty Services, Inc. remains an independent, locally owned and operated business, and it dominates the market. How did Carol Bosshardt succeed when so many others have failed?

"When I started the business in 1987, I was determined to combine a close personal relationship with employees, associates, and the people we serve with the qualities of a leading-edge professional company, and we've done that," she says. "We are the biggest real estate company in town. We have our own human resources department, an IT department, a marketing department, and the best in-house training program in the area."

In addition to its success in residential sales in the Gainesville marketplace, Bosshardt also excels in both commercial leasing and sales, and new homes and community development. What's more, through its ownership and/or partnership with Waterford Title & Insurance Co. and Alarion Bank, Bosshardt can provide "one-stop shopping" from listing and showing properties, to helping arrange financing, to closing in a timely fashion. Bosshardt also operates Bosshardt Property Management, Inc., which

> "What makes us different, I believe, is that we use all our resources to make Gainesville a better place to live."

Bosshardt Realty strives to extend its reputation for "True Customer Service" to every corner of the community. An example is Bosshardt's recently opened Campus Office, "Your real estate connection to the Gator Nation." It is located inside the Target Copy Center and food court building directly across the street from the University of Florida.

34 GAINESVILLE — EVERY PATH *starts with* PASSION

has two divisions: a leasing, management, and maintenance operation, and a community association management department.

At the core of this success is Carol Bosshardt's commitment to the company's ongoing training program, which has been dubbed "Bosshardt University." Since the company often recruits new agents from other fields, Bosshardt University gets these agents up and running within thirty days. It begins with a ten-day intensive course that gives new agents the tools, knowledge, and confidence to be successful.

"We have continuing in-house training in addition to the courses our associates take on their own," Carol says. "Approximately forty of our REALTORS® recently went through new construction 'boot camp,' where they received information about the building, design, marketing, and selling of new construction homes and neighborhoods."

Bosshardt's success in the sale of new construction is closely tied to its IT department. "Our IT group is truly remarkable," says Aaron Bosshardt, chief operations officer, who oversees the day-to-day operation of all the Bosshardt companies. "A good example is our web site, which was built specifically for us. We do so much research and can track and retrieve information so efficiently, builders often

Continued on page 36

Because Bosshardt Realty is a locally owned and operated company, all decisions are made on site by the senior managers. At least once a week Carol Bosshardt, standing at the head of the table with her son Aaron Bosshardt, seated to her right, and her daughter-in-law Kim Bosshardt, seated to her left, calls together the managers and their assistants. In addition to the broker–vice presidents, representatives from the accounting, human resources, IT, marketing, and legal departments participate in these meetings.

GAINESVILLE — EVERY PATH *starts with* PASSION 35

Bosshardt Realty Services, Inc.

PHOTO BY SCOTT INDERMAUR

Families and friends get together in the park in Haile Plantation's distinctive Park View neighborhood. Bosshardt represented and sold Park View through its New Homes and Communities Division.

Bosshardt Realty continued from page 35

come to us in the planning stages. Based on our research, they will find a site, do the building, and turn all the marketing and sales over to us."

Another advantage is Bosshardt's in-house marketing department, which produces materials from concept to design to production. "We can create campaigns for our company, our agents, and our clients," Carol says. "We produce mail-outs, print ads, brochures, postcards, and even marketing proposals."

Real estate isn't just about finding the right house. It's about bringing together families and the place they will call home for years to come. At Bosshardt Realty Services, Inc., everyone—even the children of our sales associates—is focused on one goal: to help our customers get through the sometimes complex process of buying or selling a home. Or, as our little friend likes to say, "We put out your real estate fires before they begin."

PHOTO BY SCOTT INDERMAUR

Despite all the companies and departments operating under one umbrella, Bosshardt's core values—honesty, accountability, communication and teamwork, community service, ethics, and family culture—keep everyone focused on "True Customer Service," which translates into "Customers for Life."

Because of these core values, the Bosshardt companies, their employees, and their associates are actively involved with more than one hundred charities in the Gainesville area, including Junior Achievement, the Interfaith Hospitality Network, the Gainesville Soccer Alliance, and the Tyler's Hope project. Bosshardt donates more than one hundred thousand dollars annually to local charities and nonprofits.

Paramount among the charities is the Partners in Adolescent Lifestyle Support (PALS) program. Bosshardt sponsors an annual golf tournament to benefit the program that is now implemented in four Alachua County schools.

Continued on page 38

Bosshardt's Commercial and Land Division represents the real estate interests of a number of local, state, national, and even international firms. This architecturally distinctive building is the corporate headquarters of Naylor Publishing Company. Bosshardt is paving the way to help make name-brand tenants great Gainesvillians.

GAINESVILLE — EVERY PATH *starts with* PASSION 37

Bosshardt Realty Services, Inc.

PHOTO BY GENE BEDNAREK

Bosshardt Realty continued from page 37

"We help send counselors into the schools to train the most popular kids to reach out (be a pal) to those who aren't so popular, preventing isolationism that could result in drug use, depression, and even suicide," Carol says. "Since we helped start the program, drug infractions have gone down 90 percent."

Initially Bosshardt was the sole funder of PALS. Now other grants help fund the program. Since 1999, Bosshardt has raised more than five hundred thousand dollars to benefit PALS.

In a world of chains and mega-corporations, it is nice to know that a family-owned business can prosper as a leading-edge, professional enterprise working to enhance its community.

Bosshardt's float in the University of Florida Homecoming Parade featured a giant football covered in ten thousand paper carnations handmade by the Bosshardt team. Numbers on the float riders' jerseys represented former UF players who went on to play professional football in the NFL.

"We have leading-edge technology, training, and commitment to the community," Aaron Bosshardt says. "What makes us different, I believe, is that we use all our resources to make Gainesville a better place to live. It's evident in the way we evaluate our employees, the way we provide service to our clients, and the way we give back to the community." ∎

Each year around Halloween the businesses in the Haile Village Center hold an Oktoberfest street celebration on the block in front of Bosshardt's Haile Plantation office. All the businesses hand out treats, and there are bands and a children's dance company performance sponsored by Bosshardt.

Every year Bosshardt Realty sponsors a golf tournament to benefit the PALS (Partners in Adolescent Lifestyle Support) Program, which provides peer support and therapeutic intervention to troubled students in several Alachua County schools. Bosshardt sales associates and staff spend many hours putting together the tournament and silent auction, which attracts a number of local business and community leaders.

PHOTO BY GENE BEDNAREK

GAINESVILLE — Every Path *starts with* Passion 39

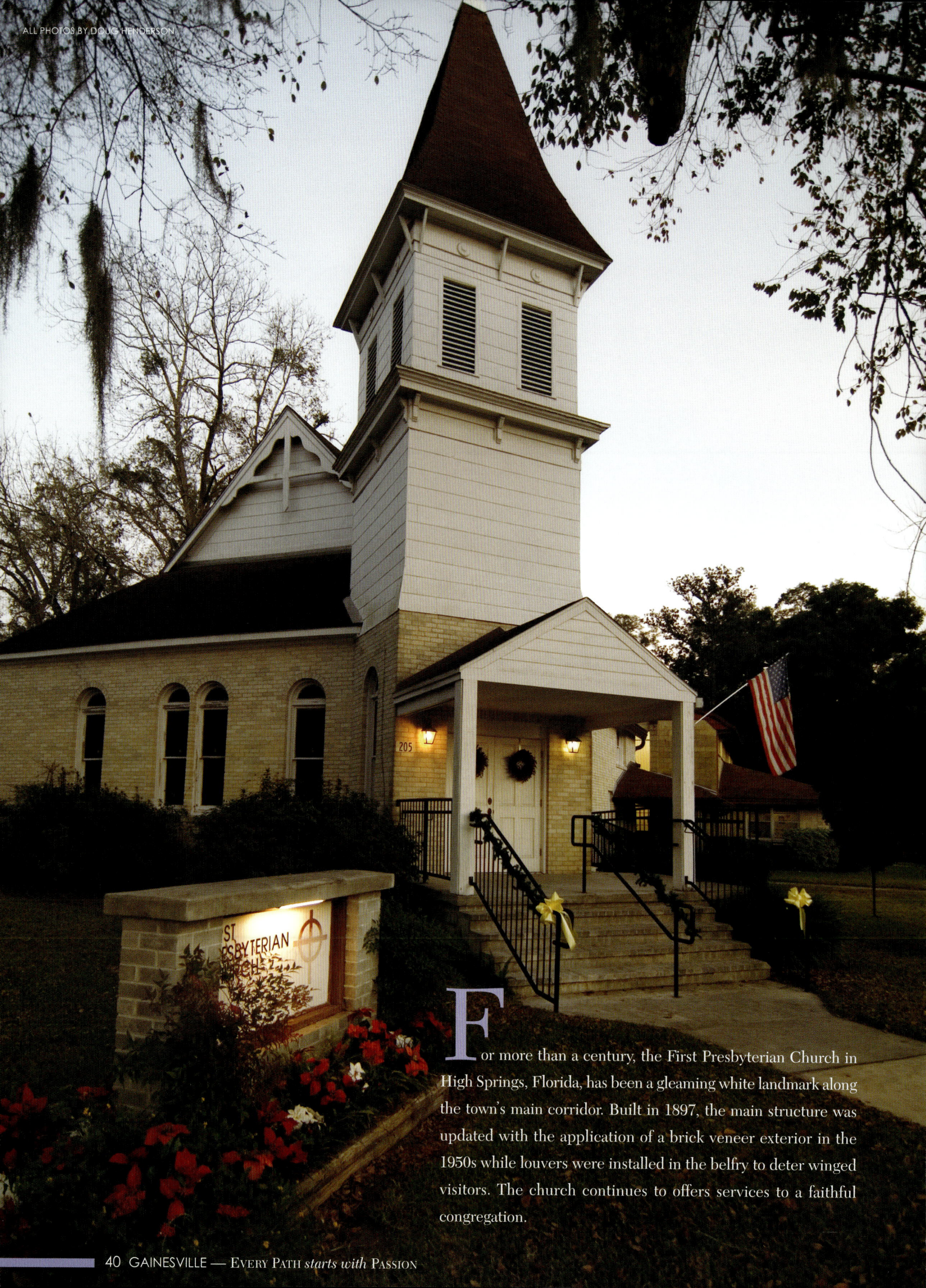

For more than a century, the First Presbyterian Church in High Springs, Florida, has been a gleaming white landmark along the town's main corridor. Built in 1897, the main structure was updated with the application of a brick veneer exterior in the 1950s while louvers were installed in the belfry to deter winged visitors. The church continues to offers services to a faithful congregation.

Patricia Hannon and a furry friend take part in the holiday fun at the Annual Twilight Christmas Parade in High Springs, voted Florida's Friendliest Small Town. The yearly family-friendly event includes food, vendors, entertainment, and a visit from jolly Santa himself. Located just up the road from Gainesville, High Springs is a place of history, outdoor enjoyment, and shady streets lined with shops.

GAINESVILLE — Every Path *starts with* Passion

Barry Rutenberg Homes

Barry Rutenberg Homes "Builds On Success"

If professional rewards signal a quality builder, then Barry Rutenberg Homes has lined up an impressive array of indicators: Rutenberg, president, is the only three-time winner of the Builders Association of North Central Florida Builder of the Year award, the only living Gainesville area recipient of the Florida Home Builders Association Builder of the Year Award, and an inductee to the Florida Housing Hall of Fame. He and his staff appreciate such recognition, but they are most pleased when their clients are delighted. To Rutenberg, repeat and referred customers make the most meaningful statement that he and his skilled associates are doing a great job. (Over the years, one satisfied customer has built nine homes with the company!)

A custom home builder who also offers modifiable inventory homes, Rutenberg has built more than a thousand homes in Alachua County since 1973, but who has time to count? He and his staff (with an average tenure of over ten years), spend their waking hours with customers—getting their feedback, listening to their ideas, and building homes based on each client's lifestyle. That attention to the buyers' needs is why the company, with its own in-house designers, is known for the functionality of its plans as well as the quality of design and construction. And Rutenberg's reputation is that of a stand-up guy who will return to a home ten years later to check into a homeowner's concerns.

"We always want to do an outstanding job for our homeowners," says Rutenberg. "We work really hard to make their dreams a reality." ■

> "We always want to do an outstanding job for our homeowners," says Rutenberg.

PHOTO BY SCOTT INDERMAUR

Barry Rutenberg stands by the pool and cabana area of a Barry Rutenberg custom home in Gainesville. He hasn't had much time for standing still, however. His company has completed more than a thousand homes since 1973—homes known for their quality construction and distinctive design.

42 GAINESVILLE — EVERY PATH *starts with* PASSION

At every Chamber After Hours, members of the Gainesville Area Chamber of Commerce have the opportunity to get to know other professionals from around the area. Hosted by members, the event is one of the many networking activities organized by the Chamber. In addition to a variety of gatherings, the Chamber helps promote its member companies through publications, a business-to-business coupon program, advertising opportunities, and more.

The distinctive Commerce Building houses the offices of the Gainesville Area Chamber of Commerce, an organization that has been a strong advocate for the area's businesses and professionals since 1924 and today touts a membership of more than fourteen hundred.

BOTH PHOTOS BY SCOTT INDERMAUR

GAINESVILLE — EVERY PATH *starts with* PASSION 43

Experience the Best of Southern Hospitality at the Best Western Gateway Grand

Jorge Negron, director of catering at Gainesville's Best Western Gateway Grand Hotel, frequently drops in at weekend wedding receptions to ensure that last-minute details are complete. However, during one Saturday reception, the wedding cake was still missing as guests arrived. Negron contacted the bride's bakery and discovered that the order had been lost and the cake had not been made! "I drove to the bakery and picked out a fake display cake so that the couple could have their pictures taken with it," said Negron. "Then I ran to the grocery and bought sheet cakes. We wheeled the fake cake to the back after the pictures were taken, and came out with the real cake already sliced. Besides the groom, bride, and mother of the bride, I don't think anyone knew that we had a fake cake at the wedding reception."

This is the type of service that the Gateway Grand provides to every guest—one of many reasons that the hotel's beautiful rooms and suites are frequently filled to capacity and its two ballrooms continually booked. "We have equal shares of people who are traveling through Florida on leisure or business travel," says Ron Gromoll, general manager, describing the diverse appeal of the property. That wide appeal is understandable to anyone who steps into the spacious two-story lobby. In fact, arriving at the Gateway Grand feels like entering a lush, countryside home, tastefully decorated and flush with luxuries. While lounging by the hotel's oversized pool or sipping a cool cocktail in the gazebo, guests

> Arriving at the Gateway Grand feels like entering a lush, countryside home, tastefully decorated and flush with luxuries.

PHOTO BY SCOTT INDERMAUR

Preparing the table settings for a special dinner is one more thing that clients of the Gateway Grand can mark off their list when planning for a big event. The hotel offers the finest conference, food, and beverage facilities, along with a professional sales and catering team to assist in planning and a service staff that ensures a flawless and elegant social or business event.

enjoy the vista of tranquil rolling hills surrounded by old Southern oaks, always complemented by a stunning sunset. One would never guess that downtown Gainesville and the University of Florida are only a few miles away.

This full-service, nonsmoking hotel is a relaxing oasis after golfing at nearby Meadow Brook Golf Course, snorkeling in the natural waters of Ginnie Springs, or visiting the Florida Museum of Natural History's Butterfly Rainforest vivarium. Just across the street, take a stroll through the Santa Fe Community College Zoo, one of only two teaching zoos in the United States. Its presence has attracted some unique guests to this pet-friendly hotel, where every cat and dog receive goody bags at check-in. With guests such as animal enthusiast Jack Hanna, the hotel has housed vultures, big cats, foxes, and giant snakes. "Many people travel with their pets, so we pride ourselves on being pet friendly," says Tammy White, director of sales. However, cleaning a room that houses a cheetah in a giant cage can be a bit challenging. "The cheetah was not happy about us being in the room, and quite honestly, while he was growling, we were not that happy being in the room either," Gromoll relates.

Of course a cheetah is the type of rare guest not interested in the hairdryer, coffee/tea maker, Wi-Fi, and complimentary

A luxury locale among Southern oaks, the Gateway Grand allows visitors the illusion of a remote villa, even though it is conveniently located moments away from the sights and sounds of Gainesville. The hotel's oversized pool and shady gazebo tranquilly await patrons who opt to indulge in a sunny day of relaxation and self-pampering.

Continued on page 46

Best Western Gateway Grand

PHOTO BY SCOTT INDERMAUR

The Best Western Gateway Grand's onsite pub is a sports-themed gathering place for hotel residents as well as the public. Honoring Florida's Gators, the Gator Den Sports Grill always serves as a relaxing venue for a cold drink, and includes tabletop televisions and eight big screens.

Best Western Gateway Grand continued from page 45

deluxe continental breakfast provided for every guest. Over half of the hotel consists of suites with king beds, separate sitting areas, spacious work areas, microwaves, and refrigerators. The Presidential Suite, one of several specialty suites, offers three bedrooms (each outfitted with exquisite furnishings), two full baths, one half-bath, dining and living areas, and a private balcony. Other specialty suites include hot tubs (several with light shows), four-poster beds, DVD players, and waterfall showerheads. Add to this the fitness center, the onsite Gator Den Sports Grill with tabletop televisions and eight big-screen sets, plus free high-speed Internet throughout the property, and an entire vacation is yours without leaving the grounds.

There is such thing as a free breakfast at the Gateway Grand, where every overnight guest receives a complimentary deluxe continental breakfast, whether they are attending a business gathering in the hotel's expansive conference and event space or heading out to enjoy the pleasures of Gainesville.

46 GAINESVILLE — Every Path *starts with* Passion

Here even business meetings feel like a holiday as the hotel staff accommodates Alachua County's growing corporate base with a free-of-charge business center for guests, a boardroom, and eight thousand square feet of conference and event space.

In keeping with the mission to provide "the best service possible to our guests, unconditionally," the staff makes every customer feel like royalty. "That's why we call it 'Grand,'" says White.

Every Best Western Gateway Grand suite features unique furniture and special amenities. This suite includes two bedrooms with king-sized beds, two full baths and one half-bath, microwave, refrigerator, and private balcony. Guests also enjoy suites with features such as hot tubs (some with light shows), waterfall showerheads, DVD players, dining and living areas, and four-poster beds.

PHOTO BY SCOTT INDERMAUR

Wedding celebrations should be perfect, as they are when arranged by the Gateway Grand. With eight thousand square feet of elegant conference and event space, the hotel provides all the services to take away the stress and create a perfect day. Professional event planners arrange catering services, set up the room, and ensure that every detail falls into place for rehearsal dinners, wedding receptions, banquets, and other special events.

GAINESVILLE — EVERY PATH *starts with* PASSION   47

48 GAINESVILLE — EVERY PATH *starts with* PASSION

BOTH PHOTOS BY MATT MARRIOTT

The University of Florida celebrated a century of football in the 2006 season. From the 1906 inaugural team, known as "Pee Wee's Boys" under coach J. A. "Pee Wee" Forsythe's direction, to the 2006 National Champion team with head coach Urban Meyer, Florida Gators football has been an adventure for generations of loyal fans. The mere mention of Florida Gators football never fails to elicit emotion. Either the arms wave wildly up and down in the now-famous "Gator Chomp," or the words "It's great to be a Florida Gator" come rolling off the tongue. If mentioned somewhere in Southeastern Conference enemy territory, other gestures and words not fit for publication might be the response. Either way, with two national championship trophies, seven conference titles, and three Heisman Trophy winners over the years, the Florida Gators have a tradition of giving football aficionados something to talk about. In 2007, the Gators were led by quarterback Tim Tebow. Nicknamed "Superman" by many because of his ability to run and gun, Tebow became the first sophomore to be awarded the coveted Heisman.

GAINESVILLE — Every Path *starts with* Passion   49

PHOTO BY GENE BEDNAREK

PHOTO BY GENE BEDNAREK

PHOTO BY SCOTT INDERMAUR

50 GAINESVILLE — EVERY PATH *starts with* PASSION

PHOTO BY SCOTT INDERMAUR

A hub for academic activity for the country's southeastern region, Gainesville offers students the area's finest educational opportunities. In addition to two dozen facilities in the public school system, educating more than thirty thousand students, Gainesville is home to Santa Fe Community College, a two-year school offering associate degrees as well as technical and vocational training. Among Gainesville's upper education institutions is the University of Florida, one of the nation's largest universities, recognized worldwide for its research activities. (Left) Nichole Blake handles instruments as part of the laboratory portion of health sciences training through Santa Fe Community College. (Bottom left page, left to right) Thomas Moore, Stephanie Dunne, Isabela Sampaio, and Rachel Cruce take their studies outdoors. (Upper left page) Students from Westwood Middle School look over the projects at Techno Building Camp, a program that gives kids the chance to build model-sized, real-world items.

GAINESVILLE — EVERY PATH *starts with* PASSION 51

UF Orthopaedics and Sports Medicine Institute

OSMI: World-Class Orthopaedics and Rehabilitation

When advanced medical science meets patient care, the result is a level of health care located only in a few premier academic health sciences centers in the world. Fortunately for the people of Gainesville, one such facility resides in the stately building that is home to the UF & Shands Orthopaedics and Sports Medicine Institute (OSMI).

One might naturally expect a learning environment in the 127,000-square-foot building, which is a modern and unique interpretation of the University of Florida's

The facility attracts patients from every Florida county, a majority of the nation's states, and several foreign countries.

Gothic architectural style. But what makes OSMI unique is that education, research, and clinical care collaborate to develop and deliver the latest innovations and treatments for bone and joint care.

"Intellectual and functional synergy is created by melding scientists, clinicians, therapists, and managers under one roof," explains Peter Gearen, MD, the institute's director. It's a forward-thinking, dynamic environment that is, in many ways, the musculoskeletal system for the University of Florida. By virtue of OSMI's comprehensive and leading-edge services, the facility attracts patients from every Florida county, a majority of the nation's states, and several foreign countries. The institute is a driving economic force.

"I'm incredibly proud, incredibly appreciative, and on a daily basis, I am humbled by what takes place here," says Les Jebson, the institute's administrative officer. Whether it's caring for an injured athlete or a farmer's hand ailment, patients are ensured of receiving world-class care, right here in Gainesville. ■

PHOTO BY DOUG HENDERSON

Chairman and director of Florida's Premier Orthopaedics and Sports Medicine Institute, Peter Gearen, MD.

Inside the walls of this Gothic building lies a hidden gem: the UF & Shands Orthopaedics and Sports Medicine Institute. OSMI treats more than one hundred thousand patients a year from all states and many foreign countries.

Town of Tioga

Town of Tioga Brings New Urbanism to Gainesville

New Orleans. Charleston. Savannah. Each of these renowned cities has something in common: they provide their residents with a genuine sense of place. They epitomize the concept of traditional neighborhood design, featuring myriad housing options, numerous recreational amenities, pedestrian-friendly streets, a town common, and more. As developers Miguel and Luis Diaz drove to, visited, and researched these cities, as well as others like them, they knew that they wanted to create that same ambience in Gainesville. And through their vision, the Town of Tioga has now joined the ranks of the country's most celebrated new urbanism communities.

"When we talk about the Town of Tioga, we have to talk about all of the things that make up the community. They're like the pieces of a puzzle, and the project is coming to fruition piece by piece," says Luis Diaz. It all started in the early 1990s, when the Diazes began purchasing land just west of I-75 with the intent of developing a community that boasts a family-first lifestyle. By the end of the millennium, development on the Town of Tioga was well under way. Today, hundreds of charming homes line the streets. While each one has a welcoming porch that serves as a focal point, what really stands out is the diversity of architecture on display. All of the houses are distinctive—just like the families that call them home.

"The kind of people you'll find here are the kind who want to belong to a community," Diaz notes. From young families to empty nesters, all demographics are represented. Although many communities segregate

> "The kind of people you'll find here are the kind who want to belong to a community."

Giving homeowners the opportunity to enjoy Gainesville's natural beauty is one of the Town of Tioga's key features. By including a linear park in the community's suite of outstanding amenities, which boasts everything from charming homes to the growing Tioga Town Center, the developers have created the best of all possible worlds, providing residents young and old with everything they need for a superb quality of life.

PHOTO BY ROD REILLY

54 GAINESVILLE — Every Path *starts with* Passion

people based on those demographics, enticing them with sections designated just for them, the Town of Tioga is a melting pot. He continues, "It's a complete mixture of people. They're all community people, and they live together in harmony."

What helps bring them together are the community's outstanding amenities, from the inviting town promenade to Tioga Town Center, the retail and commercial development at the heart of town. Throughout the year, residents take to the neighborhood's extra-wide sidewalks and head to the town common to run errands, visit the farmers market on Mondays, meet with friends, participate in community celebrations, and revel in the beauty that surrounds them. This lifestyle has earned the Town of Tioga many awards, including the 1998 ENVY Award from the Florida Association of Realtors and the Gold Award for Best Smart Growth Community in the nation from the National Association of Home Builders.

Development will continue for at least another decade, but the Town of Tioga has already made its mark in Gainesville. "It's like no other," Diaz concludes. "It really is quite a jewel." ■

Tree-lined streets with wide sidewalks are a hallmark of the Town of Tioga. They also are the perfect complement to the architecturally stunning homes that have been attracting residents to the community for years. In fact, the combination of all of these elements makes the town the perfect setting for families of all sizes.

BOTH PHOTOS BY GENE BEDNAREK

With age comes wisdom. In Gainesville, it also comes with the unique opportunity to participate in the Annual Gainesville Senior Games, hosted by the Gainesville Sports Commission in association with the City of Gainesville Division of Parks, Recreation, and Cultural Affairs. The four-day October event brings together active seniors to demonstrate their athletic skills in twelve exciting competitions, from archery, basketball, cycling, and golf to table tennis, swimming, and track and field. Nearly three hundred athletes showed their dexterity at venues throughout Alachua County in 2007, the seventh year the commission presented the Games. Their athleticism and sportsmanship were an inspiration, proving that the spirit of competition is alive and well in people of all ages.

56 GAINESVILLE — Every Path *starts with* Passion

PHOTO BY ALAN S. WEINER

Gainesville residents will recognize the colorful mural that identifies the Unified Training Center. The UTC is a multipurpose rental facility that hosts weekly classes, weekend workshops, special events, and private parties. Two students proudly demonstrate what they are learning in one of the several martial arts—and dance—programs offered. The schedule includes classes taught by the Tallest Tree Chuong Nhu Center, the Florida Fencing Academy, Aikido of Gainesville, Tribal Style Belly Dancing, Salsa Dance Class, and the Gainesville Taekwondo Academy.

GAINESVILLE — EVERY PATH *starts with* PASSION 57

Alachua County Biotech Industry

Gainesville Biotechnology Industry: Working to Help People Lead Healthier Lives

The Gainesville area boasts one of the fastest-growing life-science industry clusters in the country, with over forty-five biotechnology, medical device manufacturing, and medical research companies making Alachua County their home. Collectively, this sector employs tens of thousands of people—one of the state's most educated workforces—all working to help others lead healthier lives.

The companies in this thriving industry are supported by an extensive collection of research and commercialization-focused entities, which include the University of Florida (UF), ranked among the nation's top schools for research, patents, and licensing income, and UF's Sid Martin Biotechnology Incubator, which combines the customized resources of the incubator facilities with connections to financial backers and professionals with the know-how to foster the growth of young bioscience companies.

Of particular note among Gainesville's thriving life-sciences industry are innovators like NovaMin Technology Inc. (NTI), a company dedicated to improving oral health. NTI is working with oral care product marketers around the world to add its patented new active ingredient to existing dental products and toothpaste brands in an international effort to battle tooth decay and oral health issues. This revolutionary new ingredient, which amplifies the body's own protection and repair mechanisms in the

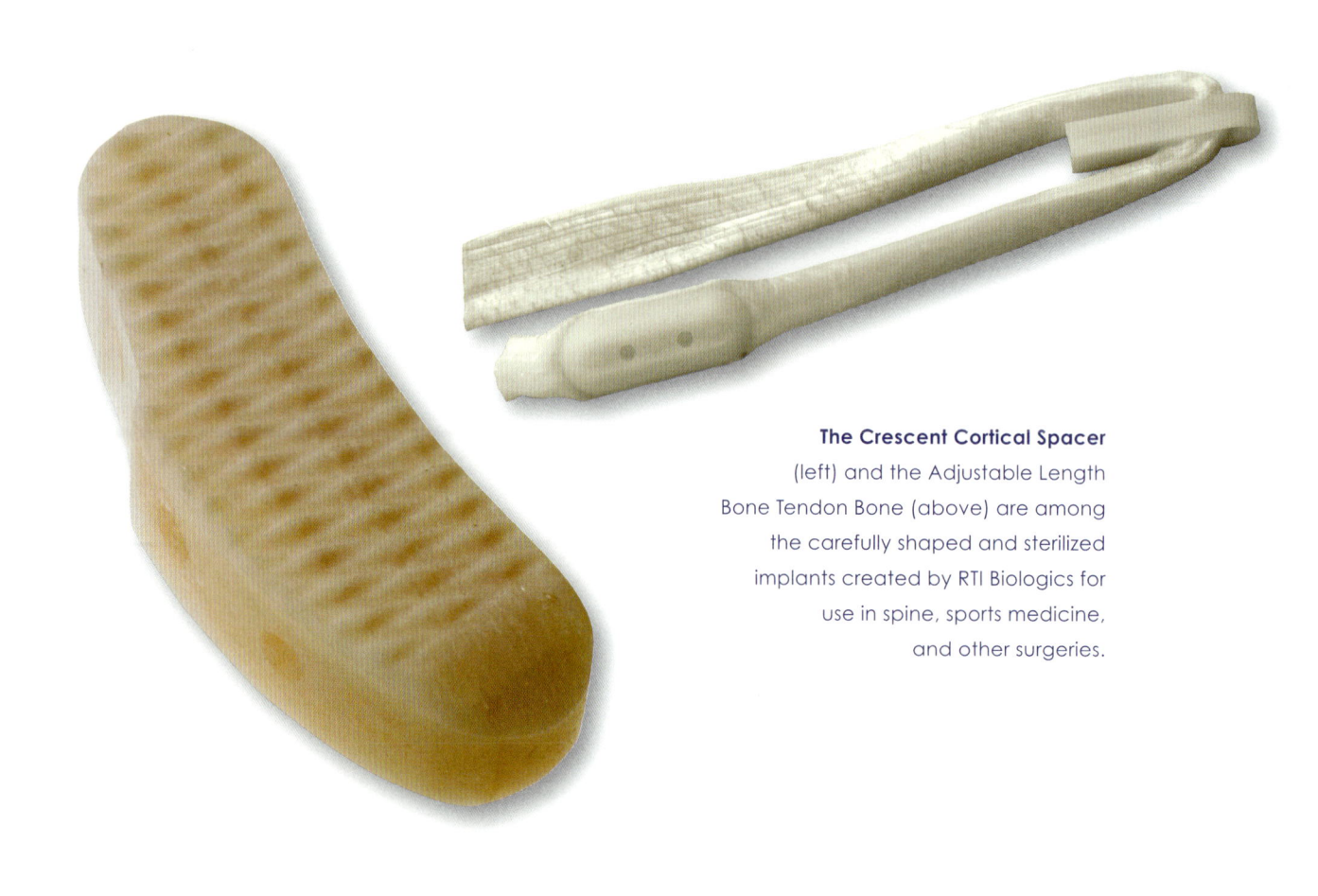

> *Collectively, this sector employs tens of thousands of people—all working to help others lead healthier lives.*

The Crescent Cortical Spacer
(left) and the Adjustable Length Bone Tendon Bone (above) are among the carefully shaped and sterilized implants created by RTI Biologics for use in spine, sports medicine, and other surgeries.

mouth, is already reshaping the industry.

Another company, RTI Biologics, prepares human-donated tissue and bovine tissue for transplantation through extensive testing and screening, precision shaping, and proprietary sterilization processes including BioCleanse®, one of the only sterilization technologies proven to eliminate donor-to-recipient transmission risk without compromising tissue strength and biocompatibility. RTI Biologics' implants are used in spine, sports medicine, and other surgeries and have proven to be very effective in repairing and promoting the healing of a wide variety of bone and other tissue defects.

Harnessing the power of the genetic code to treat human disease for which no adequate treatment currently exists is the work of Applied Genetic Technologies Corporation (AGTC). With intellectual property licensed from the University of Florida, AGTC is developing unique therapies using the nonpathogenic adeno-associated virus. Patients expected to benefit from the

Continued on page 60

Scientist Dave Knop of Applied Genetic Technologies Corporation (AGTC) attaches a probe used to monitor and control pH in a mammalian cell bioreactor. AGTC uses cells grown in bioreactors to produce safe modified viruses that are purified and formulated into products to treat human disease.

Alachua County Biotech Industry

Opened in 1995 and named after a respected state representative, the Sid Martin Biotechnology Incubator provides space, equipment, and support for the area's biotech startup businesses. In addition to providing access to wet labs, scientific instrumentation, and office facilities, the incubator helps connect entrepreneurs, financial backers, and experienced professionals.

> "Florida's achievements in the biosciences are extraordinary. As BioFlorida leads a statewide effort to further advance this momentum—and strengthen our resources—we encourage other key players to join our organization as advocates for an industry that is enhancing quality of life worldwide."
>
> —Russell Allen, President & CEO BioFlorida, Inc.

BIOFLORIDA

Florida's independent statewide trade association for the bioscience industry
www.bioflorida.com

BioFlorida commends these Gainesville area bioscience research & development and manufacturing member companies who continue to shape the future of Florida's bioscience industry.

- Applied Genetic Technologies Corporation
- AxoGen
- Banyan Biomarkers
- EcoArray
- InterMed Biomedical Services
- Nanotherapeutics
- NovaMin Technology
- Oragenics
- OxThera
- Pasteuria Bioscience
- Pegasus Biologics
- RTI Biologics
- Xhale

Formed to advance Florida's life sciences industry, BioFlorida provides companies with the necessary resources to succeed, and a strong presence both locally and internationally.

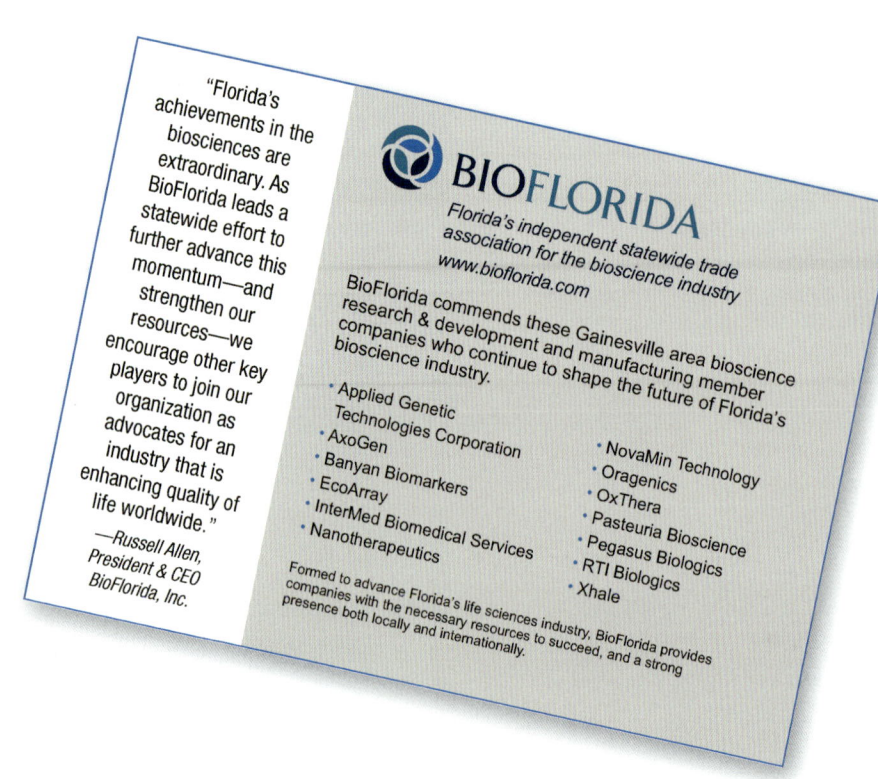

Alachua County Biotech Industry continued from page 59

company's AAV gene therapy work are those with blindness and others with a potentially fatal, inherited form of emphysema. Other health issues AGTC is targeting with its research include an inherited, muscle-weakening enzyme deficiency; an inherited deficiency producing early blindness; and a treatment for a form of macular degeneration.

Providing an information and idea exchange infrastructure for the industry is BioFlorida, an independent, statewide bioscience organization involved in networking, programs, education, and legislative advocacy. BioFlorida works with companies, investors, universities, and economic development agencies to advance commercialization opportunities and to launch start-ups, expand existing business, and attract new interests, efforts that aid the area's life sciences sector and help ensure that the world grows healthier every day. ∎

The relevance and heroism of our firefighters can never be overstated, and for over a decade the Firefighter Combat Challenge has demonstrated the value of these brave men and women. Representatives from hundreds of U.S. and Canadian municipal fire departments gather annually in twenty-five locations to compete publicly in simulated challenges that they face in real life throughout the year. With a goal of encouraging and recognizing firefighter fitness and giving the public a small glimpse into the demands of this profession, the challenge links a series of tasks, including wearing full gear and breathing apparatus while rescuing a life-sized, 175-pound "victim" from a five-story burning tower. The event that is televised to millions by ESPN includes a Kids' Firefighter Challenge, which allows children to race while wearing fire gear, and teaches them the importance of physical fitness and fire safety. Here, members of Gainesville's Fire and Rescue team show their prowess during the rescue feat, and Cary Williams, fireman, shares some professional firefighting tips with Emily Handy.

BOTH PHOTOS BY SCOTT INDERMAUR

GAINESVILLE — EVERY PATH *starts with* PASSION

Compass Bank Promises "Just a Little Bit Better" Service

"At Compass, we strive to provide service with integrity as we work with our clients on a personal level, building trust in the process. We come up with new ideas and creative ways to work a little bit harder, to be a little bit different, in order to be a little bit better. We've been able to deliver on that promise," explains Stephen B. Mitchener, Gainesville city president and Florida regional executive.

> Compass' greatest impact is on "our willingness and ability to work for the ultimate success of our clients."

Apparently Compass customers agree. Prior to becoming a wholly owned subsidiary of Banco Bilbao Vizcaya Argentaria in September 2007, Compass Bancshares ranked among the top thirty U.S. bank holding companies by asset size and among the top earners of its size based on return on equity. As one of forty-four offices in Florida, the Gainesville banking center concentrates on commercial, industrial, and private banking, and is committed to a strategy of reinvestment in the community. "We have a professional team of bankers who are quick to respond to the needs of our clients. Compass has all the services of a global bank. Those services are personally delivered by competent bankers ready to go to work on the financial needs of our customers," says Mitchener.

Compass gives back to the community through substantial financial donations to civic and charitable organizations, as well as time donated by many of the employees to those organizations. While these direct contributions are significant, Mitchener feels Compass' greatest impact is on "our willingness and ability to work for the ultimate success of our clients, thus benefiting the community at large." ∎

PHOTO BY SCOTT INDERMAUR

(Left to right) David Wilson, Gainesville corporate banking manager; Andy Hardin, regional private banking manager; and Steve Mitchener, Gainesville city president and Florida regional executive, discuss ways in which Compass Bank remains "Just a Little Bit Better." "One of the ways we do this," says Mitchener, "is by taking the extra steps to ensure our clients they are our first priority and that we will work for them. For when they are successful, we are successful."

PHOTO BY ROD REILLY

This serene scene of Gainesville's city hall and the calming sounds of a fountain surrounded by tropical palms testify to the many faces of the city, because nearby in Gainesville's renovated historic district and surrounding areas, the streets are abuzz almost around the clock. Food, music, and shopping are major attractions, with a full menu of each. Gainesville's hundreds of restaurants range from cafeteria style to coat-and-tie, from barbecue to Vietnamese. In fact, one would find it difficult to discover an ethnic food that isn't represented here, where settings range from a casual booth in a diner to white-tableclothed seating on a romantic lakefront. With forty-five shopping centers (one a renovated million-square-foot enclosed mall), and endless small shops and boutiques, shopaholics indulge their addiction, while fun-seekers choose from numerous activities such as a trolley trip or a horse-drawn downtown tour. Live bands of every kind, from reggae to rock, appeal to music lovers, with plenty of room for dancing in this city that is all about choices.

When the school day lets out, a certain group of students from Eastside High School hits the water instead of the road. That's because they are members of the oldest high school rowing club in Alachua County, one of the flagship clubs of Gainesville Area Rowing (GAR). The nonprofit organization was created to promote rowing as a sport for high school students, teaching them physical fitness and nutrition and instilling in them the psychological and mental skills they'll need to succeed in all aspects of life. Each spring, which is known as "sprint race season," the young GAR members compete in regattas throughout Florida, allowing the talented and dedicated athletes to demonstrate their skills against some very worthy opponents. And when they're not working together to propel their boat through the water to a win, they're training and practicing, spending time out on the lake, even as the sun goes down. It's that type of commitment that ultimately will lead them to victory—as a team and as individuals.

ALL PHOTOS BY SCOTT INDERMAUR

GAINESVILLE — E*very* P*ath* starts with P*assion* 65

Crime Prevention Security Systems and Custom Home Entertainment: Technology for Living

Gainesville businessman John Pastore is passionate about supporting nonprofit organizations like the Boys and Girls Club of Alachua County and the Children's Home Society. As the founder and president of Crime Prevention Security Systems, it seems only natural that Pastore would donate time, treasure, and talent to charities that have at the heart of their missions the basic human need on which he founded his first company: the need for security.

"These organizations are about helping provide a sense of security for children. We're keeping them off the streets through planned programs, and we're helping many of them find permanent homes," explains Pastore.

Pastore began installing basic alarm systems part-time while attending school back in 1975. By 1980, there was enough business to launch Crime Prevention Security Systems (CPSS) full-time. Today, the business is one of the area's largest providers of life safety and security systems. It is also one of the only locally owned security companies in North Central Florida that provides monitoring service through their own central monitoring station. A second company, Custom Home Entertainment, evolved in the new digital age as technology advanced and interest grew for integrated solutions such as structured wiring, surveillance cameras, whole-house distributed audio, central vacuum systems, and surround-sound home theaters.

GE Security has the advertising slogan "Security Is a Family Matter," and Pastore's

> Today, the business is one of the area's largest providers of life safety and security systems.

Crime Prevention Services and Custom Home Entertainment is truly a family-run business that walks the walk. Founder John Pastore and his family relax at home using their Control 4 Home Automation System.

PHOTO BY DOUG HENDERSON

companies reflect this notion. Randi Elrad, Pastore's wife, has played a vital role in the business since the beginning. As vice president of sales, she manages a team of system designers who are constantly educating themselves on the latest innovations for security and home entertainment. Daughters Jorgia McAfee and Jessica Pastore joined to manage operations and marketing, respectively. Son-in-law Bobby McAfee oversees graphic design, multimedia, and training support. Pastore believes that having family involved further strengthens the underlying vision to be large enough to serve the customers, but small enough to care.

"We're one of the largest integrators in the country, yet we have that small-company mentality where we believe the customer is the boss. Having family involved in the business allows us to keep the focus on our goals and keep the company in check," he says.

A look inside the Crime Prevention Security Systems and Custom Home Entertainment building on SW Thirty-fourth

Continued on page 68

It takes a terrific team to make a company successful, and the entire Crime Prevention team embodies that spirit.

GAINESVILLE — EVERY PATH *starts with* PASSION 67

Crime Prevention Security Systems and Custom Home Entertainment

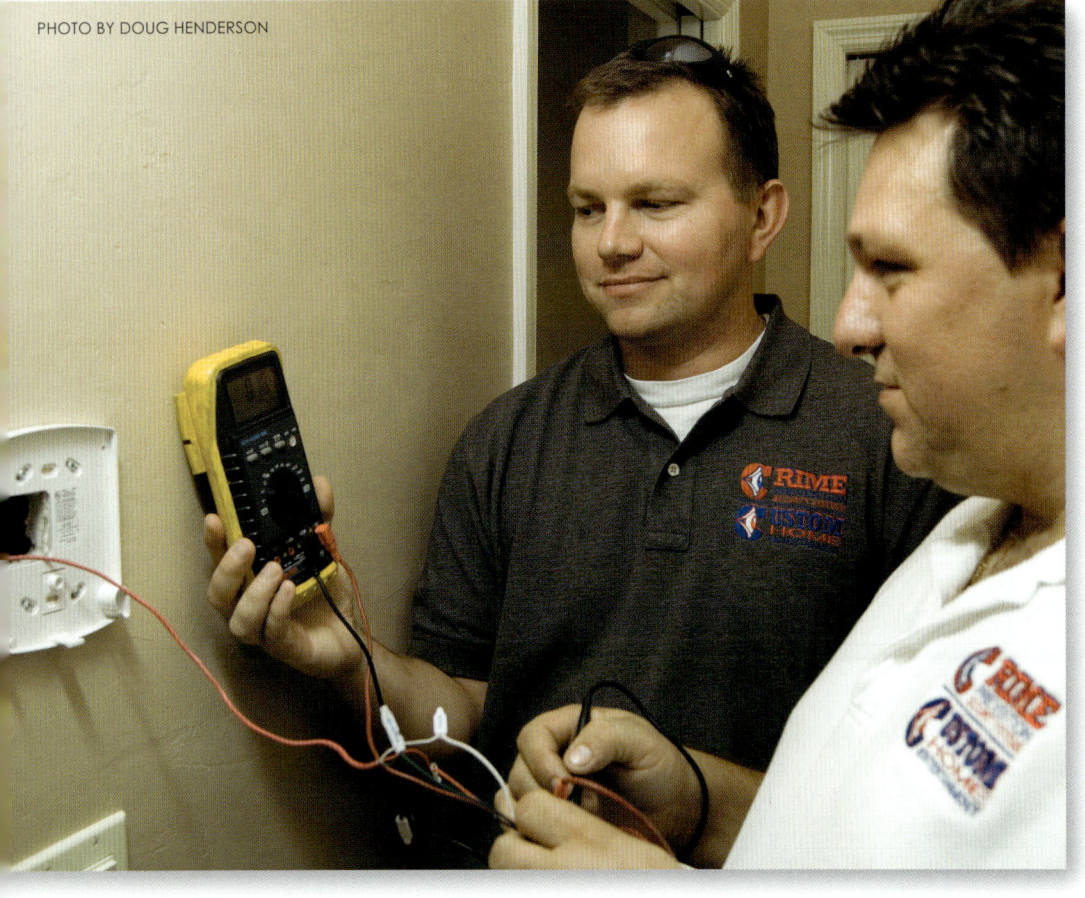

PHOTO BY DOUG HENDERSON

One way Crime Prevention Security Systems sets itself apart is the fact that it is full service—from sales to installation. Lead technicians Alan Wooten (left) and Marshall Sims (right) have the requisite expertise to troubleshoot the installation of a new security keypad.

CPSS continued from page 67

Street in Gainesville may feel like a glimpse into the future, but as Pastore and his team will tell you, that future is now. "Technology is moving very quickly," he says. "The exciting part is that through our affiliation with the Authorized Integrators Network and GE Home Technologies, we've been able to stay on the cutting edge."

In their home technology showroom, customers can get hands-on demonstrations of security, home automation, and the latest home entertainment solutions. From home/office networking to home security to home theater, homeowners can envision a world of whole-house possibilities and a new standard in enjoyment, comfort, and communication.

Randi Elrad, vice president of sales/owner, leads the weekly sales meeting. Team members stay on top of trends in the industry to ensure that the company remains both a leader and an innovator.

PHOTO BY SCOTT INDERMAUR

68 GAINESVILLE — Every Path *starts with* Passion

PHOTO BY DOUG HENDERSON

As proud as he is to have his family working alongside him, and believing in the business as much as he does, Pastore is equally as proud of the reputation of the two companies. "Since the beginning, we've understood the importance of building a solid reputation in the communities we service," he says. By forming partnerships with the best manufacturers in the industry, CPSS and Custom Home Entertainment have both been able to guarantee quality products. And through a committed and loyal staff of experts, the companies have been able to consistently deliver quality workmanship.

"The feedback we get from our customers is that we do what we say we're going to do," Pastore adds. "That's our commitment, and that's what's helped us remain successful through the years." ∎

Customers can see, touch, feel, *and* experience the range of products in this state-of-the-art entertainment and security showroom.

The day begins early at Crime Prevention Security Systems and Custom Home Entertainment. The familiar white vans with the red and blue logo can been seen on the roads and at businesses and residences throughout North Central Florida.

PHOTO BY SCOTT INDERMAUR

GAINESVILLE — EVERY PATH *starts with* PASSION 69

70 GAINESVILLE — Every Path *starts with* Passion

Ask any soccer mom, and she will quickly tell you that soccer is the fastest-growing youth sport in America. In a true community effort between the Gainesville Soccer Alliance (GSA), local banks, the Alachua County Commission, and a host of volunteers, the thirty-acre Jonesville Field of Dreams project became a reality. Using these six tournament-sized soccer fields, the GSA will continue to promote competitive youth soccer by providing licensed coaches, professional instruction, and a commitment to sportsmanship, teamwork, and personal development. The GSA will manage the fields and concessions, but they will belong to the people of Alachua County to use as individuals or rent from the club. Bordering the fenced soccer fields are warm-up grass fields, which are great places to picnic or simply unwind and cool off after a hard match.

ALL PHOTOS BY GENE BEDNAREK

GAINESVILLE — EVERY PATH *starts with* PASSION 71

Alarion Bank

Alarion Bank: Providing Hometown Banking Values

Names are important. So in 2005 when a group of investors decided to start a new bank in Gainesville, they decided to combine the names of the counties they wished to serve—Alachua and Marion—and Alarion Bank was formed. It is now one of the fastest-growing community banks in Florida—with three branches in Alachua County, three in Marion County, and more than $200 million in assets.

Alarion Bank is owned by local investors, managed by local personnel, and staffed by local employees, all serving the local area with the best customer service and the latest in cutting-edge technology.

Alarion has a full range of services, including a full-service residential mortgage department that assists new-home buyers, those looking to refinance, and seniors using reverse mortgages to supplement their income while maintaining home ownership.

"We also truly cater to small businesses," said Loralee Miller, chairman of the board of directors. "The bank's services include courier service to pick up deposits, experienced lending officers, and no cutoff times on deposits. Any customer can talk to the bank president about their needs. We take a personal interest in our customers' successes. One of the latest technologies for small businesses is remote scanning, which allows customers to scan checks at their offices and make a direct deposit."

"Other banks may offer this, but instead of sending a box with the equipment, we come out to install it, explain how to use it, and fix it if something goes wrong," says Bob Page, Alachua County bank president.

> "We take a personal interest in our customers' successes."

As part of its pledge to provide extraordinary service to clients, Alarion Bank offers Bank on Wheels, a free courier pick-up service to premier corporate customers. It is just one of many thoughtful services designed to make it easier to operate in today's business world.

BOTH PHOTOS BY DOUG HENDERSON

In an age of impersonal, automated answering machines, Alarion offers a unique service—a live, knowledgeable person to answer the phone. Customers love it. One customer said, "Not only did a real person answer my question, but they did it with a smile."

Another commented, "At some banks, you get charged to obtain a customer deposit slip. At Alarion, they'll fill it out for you."

"We hire experienced bankers and encourage them to use their best judgment to take care of customers and protect the bank," said Page. "This gives us an edge over banks that are rigid and uncaring. If we can't fill a need one way, we're flexible enough to offer alternatives."

The entire community benefits from this philosophy. In addition to financial support, Alarion offers free checking to nonprofit organizations and access to their giant LED signs to promote special events. Alarion also gives out thousands of piggy banks and works with schools to teach students the importance of saving.

On the job and in the community, Alarion Bank continues to live up to its name.

Take a close look at the smiling faces of these Alarion Bank associates. Chances are you'll recognize someone, because Alarion is dedicated to maintaining hometown banking values with local directors, management, employees, and investors.

BOTH PHOTOS BY ROD REILLY

In historic downtown Gainesville, one can enjoy nightlife into the wee hours visiting restaurants, bars, and clubs that feature live music for every taste. However, those who just want to sit around with family and friends and enjoy a free show can bring their blankets and plop down on the spacious grounds surrounding the nearby Downtown Community Plaza. The plaza is available for concerts, festivals, and church gatherings throughout the year, but every Friday night from May to October, talented local bands such as the Papercranes (ambient, indie rock) and Morningbell (psychedelic and rock) entertain the crowds as part of the "Let's Go Downtown Plaza Series." Entertainment also includes movies, dance performances, and theatre, all with the purpose of attracting families to the city for a night of fun.

74 GAINESVILLE — Every Path *starts with* Passion

PHOTO BY ROD REILLY

What better way to spend a lazy day than tubing at Ginnie Springs Outdoors? For most, the ride down the Santa Fe River starts at Devil's Spring, one of seven separate springs that daily pump millions of gallons of seventy-two-degree water into a crystal-clear pool. Shaded by centuries-old trees, Ginnie Springs also offers scuba, snorkeling, kayaking, and canoeing gear for exploring the springs and river. On land, Ginnie has some two hundred acres available for camping, hiking, and other outdoor activities.

GAINESVILLE — EVERY PATH *starts with* PASSION 75

Gainesville Area Chamber of Commerce: Making It Easier to Do Business Every Day

Every day, the Gainesville Area Chamber of Commerce works on removing some of the hurdles that make it difficult to conduct business. "We focus on activities that make it easier for a business to do business, and that's what determines our involvement," says Brent Christensen, Chamber president and chief executive officer.

Since 1924, the Chamber has worked to make the business climate in Gainesville and Alachua County one in which companies can thrive and grow. As a result, the Chamber's own success can be seen in activities like the Gainesville/Alachua County Technology and Enterprise Center (GTEC), a business incubator—formed through a partnership with other public entities—that supports the area's technology-based companies. Or look, for instance, at the program "Hire Me First," which the Chamber created with the Alachua County Schools system in answer to area employers' demands for high school graduates better prepared for the working world.

Through its Council for Economic Outreach (CEO), the Chamber focuses on economic development. "CEO is focused on three strategies: grow your own, expand what you've got, and attract new firms to the community," explains Christensen. This arm of the Chamber identifies business needs, minimizes obstacles to growth, and aids with matters such as site location and regulatory issues.

Ann Collett, CEO vice president, adds that the council's work also benefits the community as a whole. "We're bringing new jobs to the community through expansion and attraction efforts. Consequently, we're improving the quality of life for our residents by bringing in

> "We're bringing new jobs to the community through expansion and attraction efforts."

The opportunity to talk to potential customers face-to-face is one of the best reasons to participate in Chamber After Hours. The event is one of the many networking activities organized by the Chamber for its members.

PHOTO BY SCOTT INDERMAUR

PHOTO BY GENE BEDNAREK

higher wages or by creating additional opportunities for people to increase their household income."

The Chamber improves the quality of the business climate through its many member services. Pivotal among these are numerous networking opportunities. "People like to do business with people they know, so getting out and making those contacts is key," explains Sonia Douglas, Chamber vice president and chief operating officer.

In addition to networking, the Chamber offers its members educational opportunities through its Business Resource Center. The center's programs include those that touch on the needs of small business, such as peer mentoring, consultation, marketing tips, and more. Members also learn through gatherings that feature guest speakers who share their expertise on a range of topics. And leaders of today and tomorrow gain knowledge through Leadership Gainesville, one of the oldest such programs in the nation, touting well over one thousand graduates.

As an active voice in policy issues at the state and local levels, the Chamber serves as an advocate for business, continually working to make it easier for businesses to do business in Gainesville and Alachua County every day.

Every year in the fall, the Chamber recognizes outstanding businesses in the area at its Business of the Year Awards Luncheon. While selected companies are chosen as top recipients of awards, the event serves as a salute to all businesses that apply.

GAINESVILLE — EVERY PATH *starts with* PASSION 77

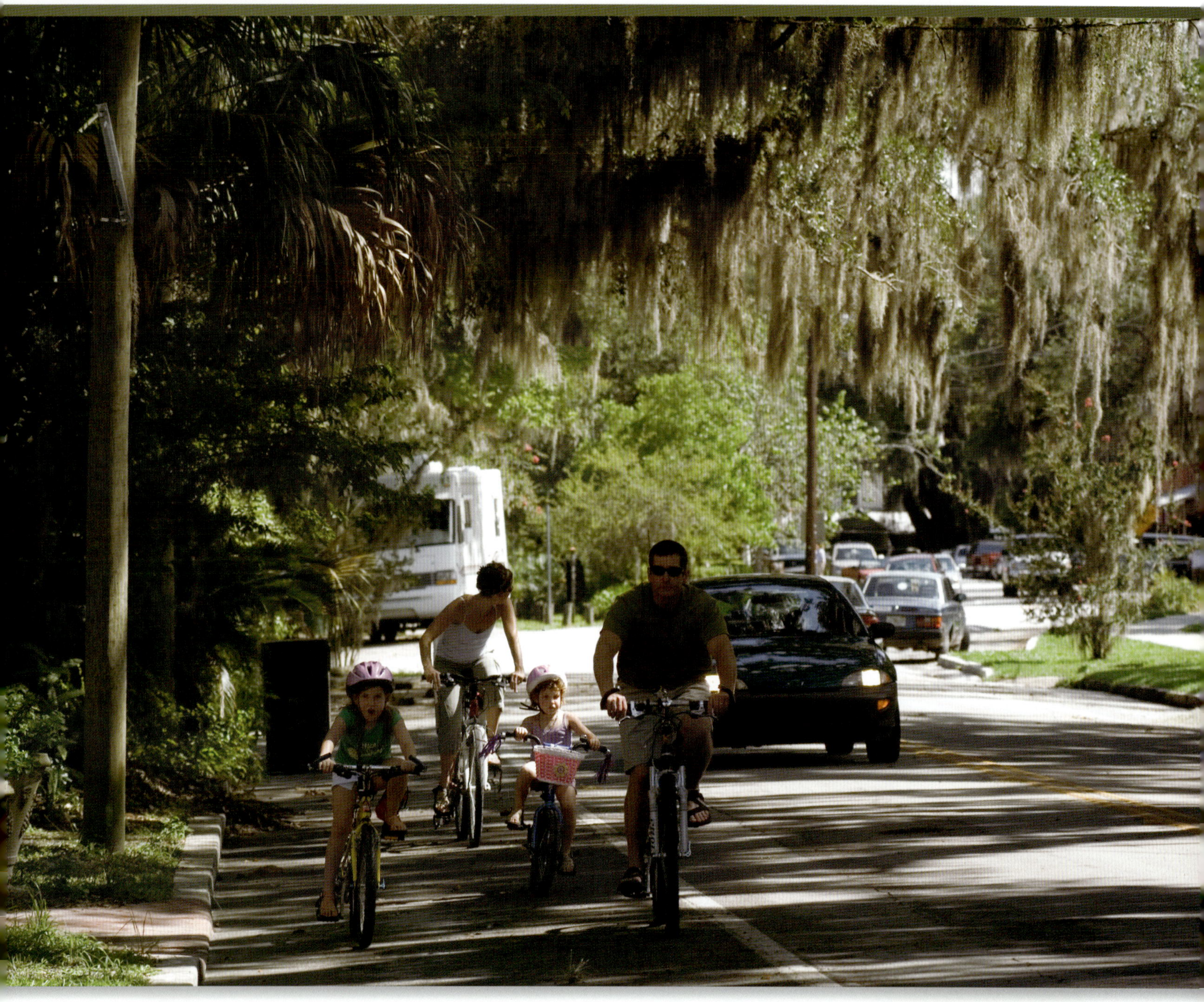

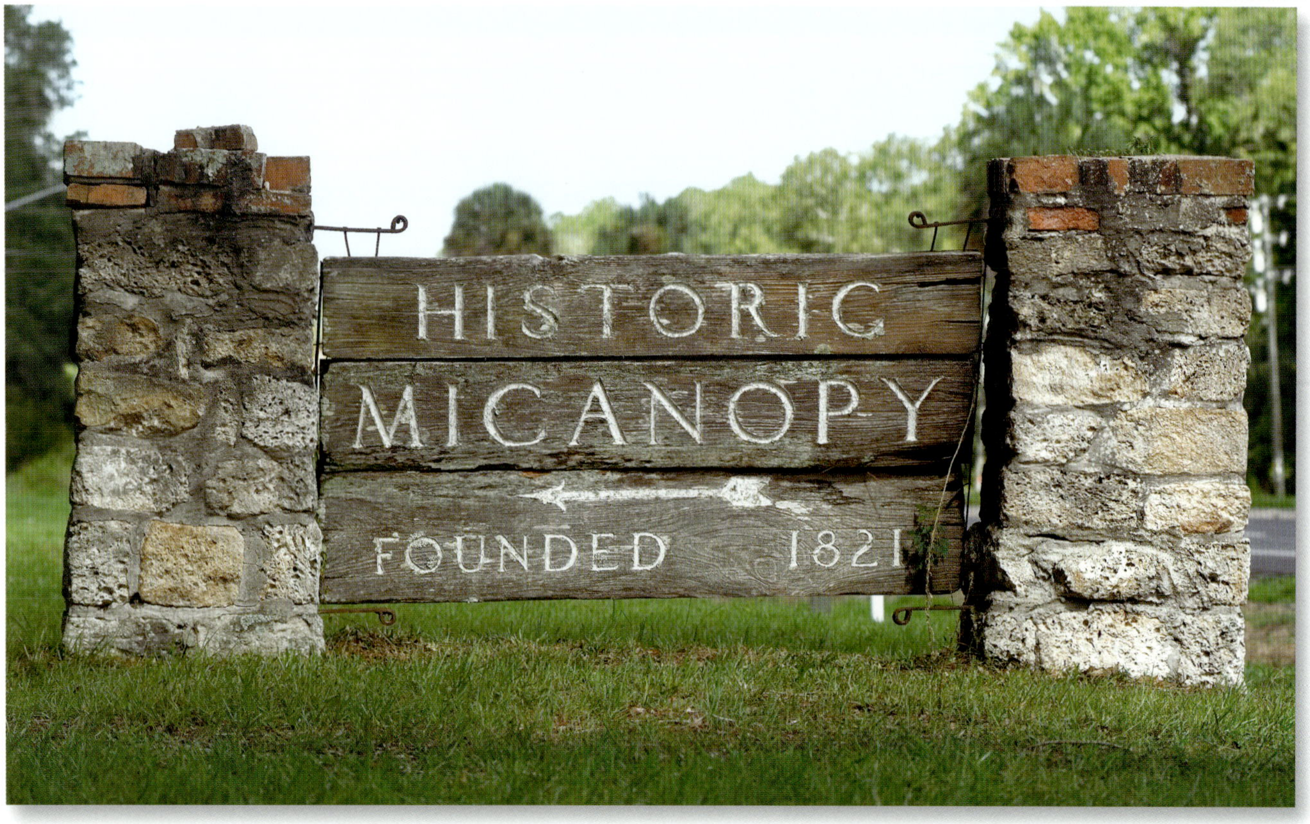
HISTORIC
MICANOPY
FOUNDED 1821

ALL PHOTOS BY ROD REILLY

Just a mile off I-75 sits the charming little town of Micanopy, the oldest inland settlement in the state. A stroll through Micanopy is like stepping back in time; its streets are lined with historic buildings, private homes, and ages-old oaks dripping with Spanish moss. Started as a settlement, then housing a fort, and even serving as the backdrop for Hollywood films, Micanopy is now a town of shops brimming with folk art, collectibles, antiques, and more.

Florida Citizens Bank

Florida Citizens Bank Is the "7 to 7 Community Bank"

Walls attributes the bank's success to a philosophy of listening to customers and implementing many of their ideas.

Florida Citizens Bank is a community bank that offers everything the big banks offer and more. "We do more than the big boys with small business checking accounts and most personal checking products," says president Carl Walls, who credits technology for giving the bank its competitive edge. "We have our own data processing center, which allows us to control what we do and how we do it."

Custom-designed software is a key to the bank's ability to operate with greater efficiency. In addition to a program that gives tellers instant access to client data, the bank's technology allows it to offer same-day credit on deposits later than other financial institutions in the area.

Technology also allows Florida Citizens Bank to tailor its offerings to meet customer requests. Known as the "7 a.m. to 7 p.m. Community Bank," Florida Citizens' extended hours have always been that way to help meet the needs of its working customers. "A long time ago I realized that, with very little effort we could be open from 7 a.m. to 7 p.m., six days a week," says Walls.

The bank has also introduced added conveniences, such as Home Banking and Bill Pay, which allows customers to pay bills in the comfort of their own abode. In addition to a full selection of personal banking options such as checking accounts and loans, Florida Citizens also offers options for people with less-than-perfect credit through New Chance Checking, a debit-card-based program that allows the cardholder to open a regular

With over sixty ATMs located throughout our market area, customers have access to their funds at any time. A number of these ATMs are in commercial locations, which allows customers to shop and do their banking in one place.

PHOTO BY DOUG HENDERSON

80 GAINESVILLE — EVERY PATH *starts with* PASSION

checking account after a year without incident.

Florida Citizens Bank also offers a full selection of unique programs that make commercial banking a breeze. Beyond loans and checking and savings accounts, the bank offers Customer Care, a spreadsheet e-mailed daily to clients that reports account activity; Remote Deposit Capture, allowing business owners to send deposits electronically with the aid of a special device; and corporate credit cards with instant credit increases and a monthly breakdown of expenditures categorized for tax purposes.

The bank's armored car service is another plus for commercial clients, taking care of daily deposits and change orders while freeing clients to continue about their workday without putting employees at risk transporting the day's receipts.

Florida Citizens Bank was formed in 1999 by a group of area investors who wanted a financial institution with local ownership. Today, Florida Citizens Bank has an asset base of some $275 million and operates eight full-service branches in Alachua and Marion counties.

Walls attributes the bank's success to a philosophy of listening to customers and

Continued on page 82

Banking done in thirty seconds.
With armored car service available seven days a week, customers never have to worry about going to the bank. An armored car driver picks up deposits and delivers cash and coin when needed.

Florida Citizens Bank

Florida Citizens Bank continued from page 81

implementing many of their ideas, a factor made easier by the bank's local ownership. "It's all about the customers," he says. "When a customer tells us they'd like a new product or service, we usually find a way to do it. We listen to them and hear what they need and try to design a package that fits, because if one person needs it, someone else may need it as well. And with local decision makers, we don't have to ask somebody in another state for permission."

No need to leave the office to make a deposit.
Through Remote Deposit Service customers can scan checks and balance deposits, and with a click send a deposit to the bank.

PHOTO BY GENE BEDNAREK

Your place or mine? Florida Citizens Bank is all about convenience for its customers. Officers often deliver documents to customers to sign or review, so they don't have to leave their business.

PHOTO BY ALAN S. WEINER

82 GAINESVILLE — EVERY PATH *starts with* PASSION

PHOTO BY GENE BEDNAREK

Rain or shine, employees are ready to serve the community. Here they sport umbrellas while waiting to treat the next group at a golf tournament with shrimp and cream puffs.

The bank also listens when the community voices its needs. While the bank contributes monetarily to numerous causes, its employees lend as much as four thousand hours of their time each year to local organizations. Serving as scoutmasters, presidents and directors for nonprofit agencies, Chamber committee members, and more, the bank's people help where help is needed. "We think it's important to help in your neighborhood," explains Walls, "because if you're going to make your money in a town, you've got to put some back in it." ■

PHOTO BY ROD REILLY

Innovation, state-of-the-art equipment, and custom-designed software allow the bank to operate with greater efficiency. Employees are pictured at the data processing center of Florida Citizens Bank, processing and balancing all the day's activity.

GAINESVILLE — EVERY PATH *starts with* PASSION 83

ALL PHOTOS BY DOUG HENDERSON

The batter's almost always up at the Newberry Sports Complex in Newberry, Florida, and the Diamond Sports Park in Gainesville, where the sounds of baseball resonate virtually year round. As part of North Central Florida Athletics, these sites attract over eight hundred teams annually as baseball lovers of all ages gather for tournaments and events such as the Winter National Baseball Invitational, King of Diamonds Youth Baseball Tournament, and the Triple Crown Sports Youth Baseball Tournament. Here (bottom right) Frank Medeiros, assistant coach of the Williston Warriors, a travel team, gives son Frankie some pitching pointers, and the Alabama Vipers (bottom left) listen to some last-minute coaching tips before both teams make some daring plays out on the field.

84 GAINESVILLE — EVERY PATH *starts with* PASSION

GAINESVILLE — E͟ᴠᴇʀʏ Pᴀᴛʜ *starts with* Pᴀꜱꜱɪᴏɴ 85

Gainesville Harley Davidson & Buell

Gainesville Harley-Davidson & Buell: Come Ride with Us

When owner/operator Gail Lytle was asked what distinguishes her business from her competitors, she answered, "We sell Harley-Davidson motorcycles!"

Right to the point. Gainesville Harley-Davidson & Buell is the only Harley dealership in town, and Harley-Davidson motorcycles are in a class by themselves. The Harley-Davidson Motor Company was founded in 1903, and still makes the same top-of-the-line product it did over one hundred years ago. It also has one of the five most recognized trademarks in the world.

"When my husband and I moved here from Michigan to start our own business, he wanted something involved with either aviation—he was a corporate pilot—or motorcycles. We wrote Harley-Davidson, got information about locations and/or available dealerships, and, as they say, the rest is history."

Gainesville Harley-Davidson opened in February 1993 in a leased five-thousand-square-foot space. Today the company owns a building, which includes a twenty-five-thousand-square-foot showroom. Lytle and her sons Paul, who is the parts manager, and Kevin, the service manager, are justifiably proud of their success.

"Harley-Davidson has a great product, the company is very supportive of their dealers, and their top executives are always available at conventions and conferences," said Lytle.

> **Harley-Davidson motorcycles are in a class by themselves.**

There are a number of theories about why Harley-Davidsons are known as Hogs. In one, a team of southern farm boys who raced Harleys consistently won races. They would take a victory lap with their mascot— a pig-riding on the back. Eventually "hog" was turned into H.O.G., for Harley Owners Group. The members of the Gainesville HOG chapter may not all believe that story, but it doesn't stop them from mounting up to enjoy the sound of a Harley and a scenic ride along Millhopper Road.

BOTH PHOTOS BY GENE BEDNAREK

86 GAINESVILLE — EVERY PATH *starts with* PASSION

"Back in the '90s, we had a waiting list for Harleys, but the company didn't rest on its laurels. They realized their customer base was getting older, so in 1998—to appeal to the younger market—they formed a partnership with Buell American Motorcycles. Harleys are cruisers, whereas the Buell is a sports bike, a street bike meant for racing."

One of the hallmarks of Harley-Davidson is customer service. Buyers are surveyed a month after the sale about their buying experience. At eighteen months, they are surveyed again about the ownership experience. The results of those surveys, plus other criteria, are used to determine which of the approximately 650 Harley-Davidson dealers in the United States will earn the gold, silver, or bronze Bar and Shield award. "We have earned nine awards over our fourteen years in business," said Lytle.

As a family-owned company, Gainesville Harley-Davidson & Buell is committed to the Gainesville area. "We support Life South, the Humane Society, the Boys and Girls Club of Alachua County, and the Children's Miracle Network, among others," said Lytle. "We also work with the local Motor Safety Foundation. To legally drive a motorcycle, you have to pass a test and get certified. The lecture portion of the classes are held at our dealership.

"When we moved here, our goal was to own our own company and do something we love," said Lytle. From all evidence, Gail, Paul, and Kevin Lytle have done just that, and they will continue to do so and to make their community better along the way. ■

Owners of Gainesville Harley-Davidson & Buell
Paul, Gail, and Kevin Lytle are justifiably proud of their dealership which—out of approximately 650 dealers in the United States—has earned nine awards based on their excellent customer service and the enduring quality of the motorcycles they sell.

GAINESVILLE — EVERY PATH *starts with* PASSION

ALL PHOTOS BY GENE BEDNAREK

88 GAINESVILLE — E‍very P‍ath *starts with* P‍assion

Everyone loves a parade. Lining the streets along the University of Florida homecoming parade route, people watch and listen for their favorites. For the traditionalists, it's the reverberating beat of the drums of the University of Florida's "Pride of the Sunshine" Fightin' Gator marching band. For about half of the university's student body, it's the cute Gator cheerleaders. Still others love the floats, representing organizations from the university as well as the community. For the kiddos, it's just about everything: the noise, the color, and the excitement. The largest student-run parade in the nation usually attracts more than one hundred thousand spectators, with another three hundred thousand watching it by live television broadcast through North and Central Florida.

GAINESVILLE — EVERY PATH *starts with* PASSION 89

Santa Fe Community College

Santa Fe Community College Enriches the Community

Santa Fe Community College's mission is to add value to the lives of its students and enrich the community. From sponsoring signature regional events such as the SFCC Spring Arts Festival to training the local workforce, Santa Fe is a vital community partner.

Founded in 1966 as Santa Fe Junior College, the college opened its campus in Northwest Gainesville in the early 1970s, and today has centers in downtown Gainesville, Keystone Heights, Archer, and Starke. Two additional facilities, the Kirkpatrick Criminal Justice Training Center and a biotech training center (opening in Alachua in 2009), provide specialized training. Complementing these sites, the online Open Campus enrolls thousands of students—further increasing access to higher education.

Santa Fe is a founding member of the League for Innovation in the Community College, the leading invitation-only community college organization, and was recently featured in *The New York Times* as an exemplary community college. With more than seventeen thousand students, Santa Fe offers degrees and certificates leading to university transfer or more than sixty different careers. Santa Fe provides many noncredit opportunities, too: Community Education, College for Kids, and PrimeTime Institute for seniors round out its educational offerings to the community.

More than 60 percent of Santa Fe's associate of arts graduates transfer to the University of Florida. Eighty percent of Santa Fe students remain in the region and contribute to the local economy, and 96 percent of graduates find careers in the field of their choice. Of the employers who have hired Santa Fe graduates,

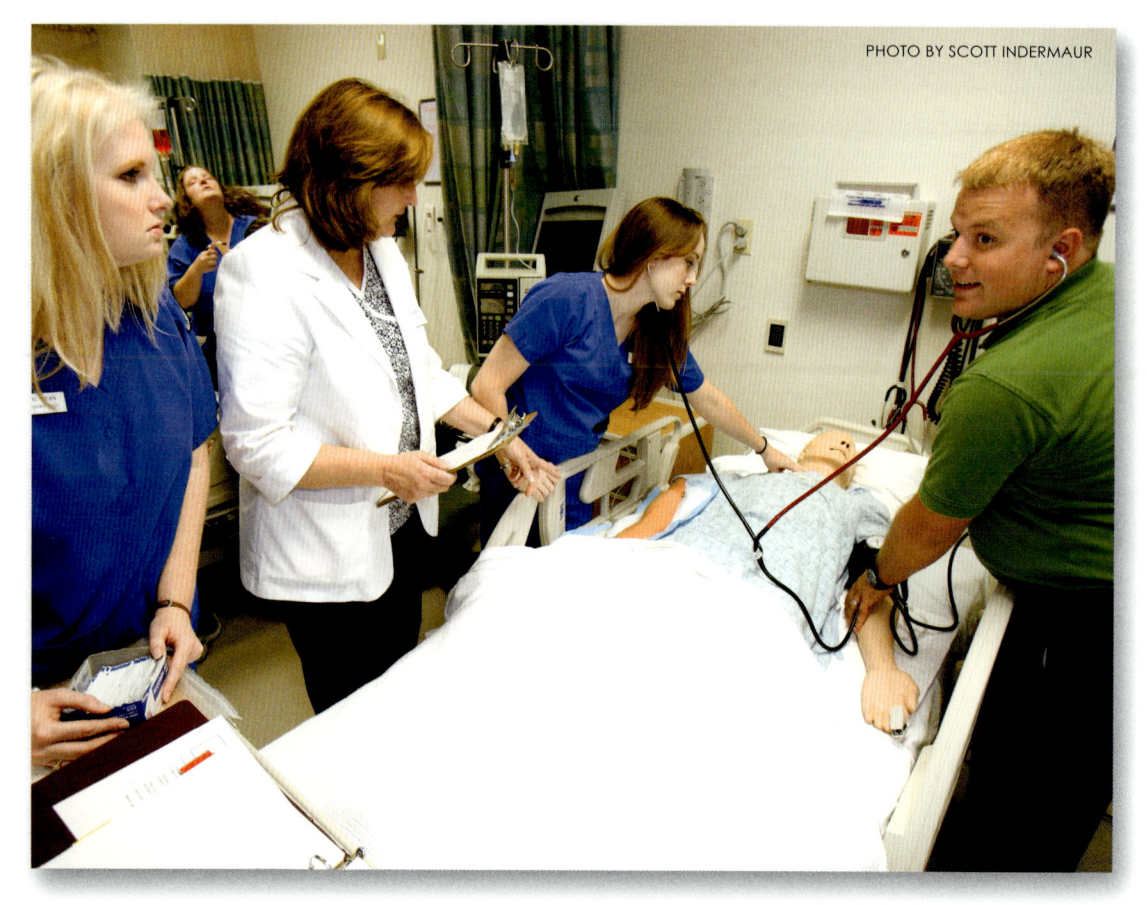

> O f the employers who have hired Santa Fe graduates, 99 percent say they would hire Santa Fe grads again.

When people in Gainesville receive medical care, chances are a Santa Fe grad is assisting them. Health Sciences programs at Santa Fe include nursing and dental assisting, along with more specialized programs such as sonography, cardiovascular technology, and surgical assisting.

PHOTO BY SCOTT INDERMAUR

99 percent say they would hire Santa Fe grads again.

When someone in Gainesville receives health care, chances are that a Santa Fe grad is involved. The graduates of the college's sixteen health science programs consistently demonstrate outstanding passing rates on state and national licensing exams. A new addition to the health sciences complex has allowed the college to expand enrollment, helping to meet the critical need for health-care professionals in Florida. The state-of-the-art facility includes patient simulators and laboratory classrooms that resemble a real-world medical facility.

Santa Fe is home to the only planetarium in North Central Florida. The Kika Silva Pla Planetarium offers weekly public shows and programs for school groups. Santa Fe's Circle of Science includes the Jean Klein Memorial Rock Cycle Garden, with twenty-two boulders from across the United States illustrating geologic development. The physical sciences building completes the circle and is home to fossil displays, laboratories, and an observation deck with telescopes for stargazing.

Santa Fe is the only community college in the country with a teaching zoo nationally accredited by the American Zoo and Aquarium Association (AZA). The zookeeper program attracts students from across the country and from as far away as Japan and Switzerland. Student zookeepers, who

Continued on page 92

Santa Fe's dance program is among the best in the southeastern United States and frequently wins in competitions with other comparable four-year school programs.

Santa Fe Community College

PHOTO BY SCOTT INDERMAUR

Students gather in the lobby of the new Health Sciences Annex, which features state-of-the-art medical labs and classrooms.

Santa Fe Community College continued from page 3

graduate with a strong focus on wildlife conservation, care for more than seventy-five native and exotic species. The zoo is open daily and welcomes more than thirty thousand visitors a year. Each Halloween, the zoo's Boo-At-The-Zoo event draws thousands of costumed children and parents, and collects donations for area food banks.

Santa Fe is the statewide Banner Center for Construction. This program trains construction managers and tradespersons in carpentry, masonry, plumbing, heating and air conditioning, and electrical. At the planned Charles R. Perry Construction Institute, students will develop their skills and a sense of community service by building cottages to serve as affordable housing.

Santa Fe takes on many large philanthropic projects each year, including the American Heart Association's HeartWalk.

92 GAINESVILLE — Every Path *starts with* Passion

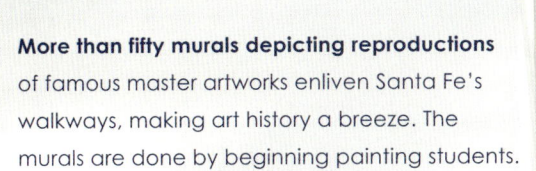

PHOTO BY SCOTT INDERMAUR

More than fifty murals depicting reproductions of famous master artworks enliven Santa Fe's walkways, making art history a breeze. The murals are done by beginning painting students.

Santa Fe's students graduate with a firm grasp of international issues. The college has an award-winning program to internationalize the curriculum, which includes study abroad opportunities. College faculty have included Alberto Alonso, co-founder of Cuban-style ballet and the subject of a college-produced documentary shown internationally, and Fulbright scholars from China and Indonesia.

The college's community outreach is exemplified by its East Gainesville Initiative. Working with faith-based organizations and community groups, EGI has installed Internet-connected computers and provided technical support for economically disadvantaged families, offered after-school tutoring and children's summer enrichment programs, and created computer labs at area churches and homeless shelters.

Santa Fe's community involvement reflects its core values. Students participate in Santa Fe's tradition of caring, and graduates leave ready to give back to the world. ■

Santa Fe is focusing on greening its campus, and recently it was selected for a pilot program that ranks sustainability practices at colleges and universities. Here, student dancers prepare to celebrate annual Campus Sustainability Day.

GAINESVILLE — EVERY PATH *starts with* PASSION 93

PHOTO BY DOM MARTINO

Formed by the merging of a collection of sinkholes, the prairie basin at Paynes Prairie Preserve State Park contains more than eight hundred plant types. American lotus is just one of the multitudes of flowering species in the basin, which join with grasses and other plants to serve as a purifying filter for the wetlands. The basin drains into underground layers and acts as a recharging system for the Floridan Aquifer, supplier of the area's drinking water.

PHOTO BY DOUG HENDERSON

One-third of all patients treated at Shands at the University of Florida are infants or children. In North Central Florida, Shands offers the only Level III Neonatal Intensive Care Unit and pediatric trauma services. Pediatric health care is offered in six Shands hospitals and more than a dozen University of Florida physician outpatient practices.

Shands HealthCare

Shands HealthCare: The Best That Medicine Has to Offer

Shands HealthCare's philosophy is unwavering: to provide outstanding, quality health care; help improve overall community health; and support the academic and public service missions of the University of Florida Health Science Center. Shands comprises two academic medical centers, two specialty hospitals, four community hospitals, and more than eighty affiliated University of Florida outpatient clinics in which UF faculty physicians practice. While the not-for profit health-care system's primary community is North Central and Northeast Florida, its reach extends far beyond that.

"We have a long-standing reputation as one of the Southeast's most respected health-care organizations," says Timothy Goldfarb, CEO. "We're proud to be Florida's leading system for patient referrals and one of the only health-care organizations that treats people from every county in the state. However, people also come to us from across the nation and more than a dozen other countries each year to access our specialized services and highly regarded medical staff."

The collaboration between Shands and UF results in the advancement of research

Shands understands that excellence depends on a commitment to serve and offers the very best, every day.

Shands Rehab Hospital— North Central Florida's only academic rehabilitation and physical medicine hospital—ranks as one of the top nationally for patient-satisfaction scores. Comprehensive inpatient and outpatient services include vocational rehab, psychological care, and occupational, recreational, physical, and speech therapy.

PHOTO BY DOUG HENDERSON

PHOTO BY DOUG HENDERSON

and education in the health sciences and outstanding patient care—in other words, "the science of hope." Not only does Shands enhance health in its communities and help influence medical science on a larger scale, but as a corporate citizen the organization also has a profound economic impact in Florida. In addition, Shands remains acutely attuned to the unique needs of underserved and under- or uninsured populations, providing millions of dollars of free or discounted health services.

Shands, its UF faculty and community physicians, and more than thirteen thousand employees provide extraordinary care to patients who turn to them for the full spectrum of health services, from primary to highly complex care. Shands understands that excellence depends on a commitment to serve and offers the very best, every day, for each and every patient. In some communities, where Shands is the only provider of hospital-based health care, this responsibility as a dedicated health-care resource is even more important.

"We're excited about the future and are fully engaged in meeting the region's increasing needs for health care now and for decades to come," says Goldfarb. "By continuing to deliver outstanding care, train the best health professionals, make breakthrough discoveries, and lead health outreach and prevention initiatives, we not only expand the science of hope, we also improve the quality of life in our communities. And from the beginning, that has been our motivation." ■

Shands's cancer patients, their family members, and caregivers painted the ceramic tiles on this Healing Wall. One of every seven adult patients hospitalized at Shands at the University of Florida has a cancer-related condition. The state-of-the-art, five-hundred-thousand-square-foot Shands at UF Cancer Hospital is designed to meet the region's increasing needs for oncology care now and for the future.

GAINESVILLE — EVERY PATH *starts with* PASSION 97

98 GAINESVILLE — *Every Path starts with Passion*

ALL PHOTOS BY ROD REILLY

On 160 rolling acres in Alachua County, the Canterbury Equestrian Showplace features five show barns, three outdoor rings, four cross-country courses, warm-up areas, and some of the most beautiful scenery in North Florida. At the College Bound Invitational Horse Show, college coaches and high school students with an equestrian interest come together in a nonthreatening, educational, competitive environment. Riders can take home great prizes like scholarships, riding clothes, and saddles, but more important they gain invaluable information they can use to plan their future college careers.

GAINESVILLE — EVERY PATH *starts with* PASSION 99

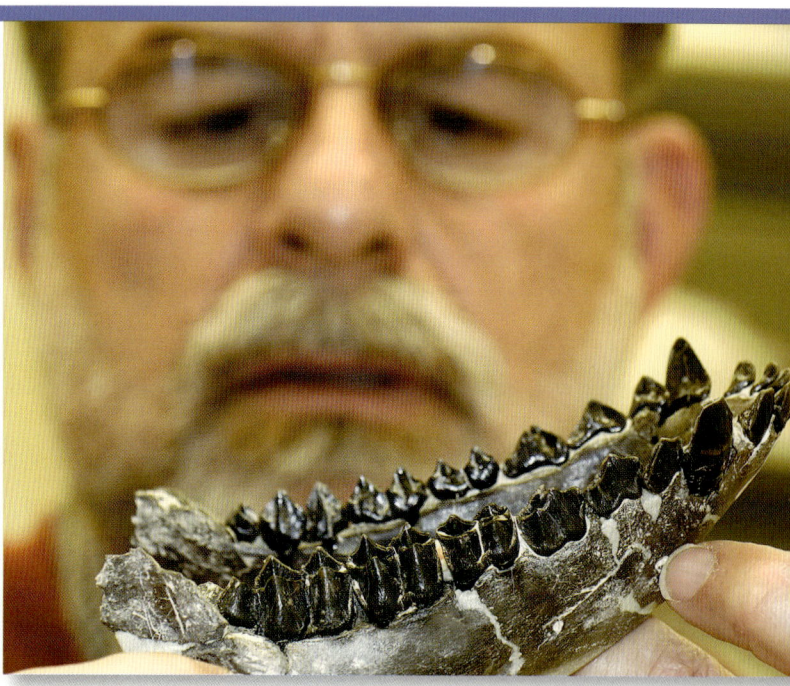

As one of the nation's most comprehensive research institutions, the University of Florida is home to many world-class research programs, including the Genetics Institute (top left); air, land and sea robotics programs (bottom); and the acclaimed Florida Museum of Natural History (top right).

PHOTO BY DOUG HENDERSON

ShandsCair provides emergency transport by ground and air for more than eighteen hundred patients every year and includes special flight teams for neonatal patients and organs for transplantation. Shands at the University of Florida has North Central Florida's only Level I Trauma Center and a regional burn center.

Brame Architects

Brame Architects: A Century of Shaping the Gainesville Built Environment

Tracing its origins back to 1911, Brame Architects has garnered a legacy of crafting the Gainesville built environment. It is a long heritage built on a foundation of contented clients.

"Our firm has always made a diligent effort to provide a personalized professional service, and to do whatever it takes to assure our client's satisfaction," says owner William W. "Billy" Brame, AIA. "We want the experience to be such that if that client ever needs architectural services again, they will come back to our firm."

During its long history, only two members of the same family have worked at the firm: founder Newbold Goin and his son, Sanford, who took over the firm in 1935. The firm was named Moore, May and Harrington when Brame came on board in 1973. Within a few years of joining the firm, Brame became a partner and, through a series of name changes and retirements, now remains its sole owner.

In addition to client satisfaction, throughout its history, Brame has retained a tradition of taking on all types of jobs. "Our firm undertakes a wide variety of projects, from small to large, simple to complex," says Brame. "We have done small remodeling efforts as well as massive, multibuilding complexes—from something as simple as a garage to a sophisticated scientific laboratory."

Among the projects in Brame's portfolio are the Gainesville Regional Airport Terminal building and the Stephen C. O'Connell Center at the University of Florida, as well as other governmental administrative buildings, office buildings, educational facilities at all grade levels, churches, condominiums, and single- and multifamily residential properties.

With each of its works, Brame takes an in-depth look at the client's needs.

The home of Saliwanchik, Lloyd & Saliwanchik is one of the area's landmarks created by Brame Architects. The two-story, 23,822-square-foot structure features a central atrium lobby area, complete with glass roof, while partner offices are located at each of the building's corners.

102 GAINESVILLE — Every Path *starts with* Passion

The firm's special expertise also encompasses historic preservation.

With each of its works, Brame takes an in-depth look at the client's needs. "In order to understand their goals and objectives, we quantify the specific activities and the spaces they require through a formal programming effort," says Brame. "We ask detailed questions that sometimes go deep into the workings of the operation or activity."

As a result of its culture geared toward relationship building, Brame has earned repeat business from some clients for as long as thirty years or more, and its staff includes people who have been on board for more than two decades.

In return for the loyalty the community has given the firm, Brame Architects shares its talent with various public and private boards, committees, and organizations such as Rotary International, assuming leadership positions whenever needed. This giving back is just one way Brame Architects will continue to be an integral part of the Gainesville landscape into a second century. ■

The Naylor Publications building is a four-story, 56,710-square-foot structure that houses the administrative and sales offices for a company specializing in association magazines and promotional literature. As per the client's wishes, Brame Architects created a high-quality facility that demonstrates the importance of personnel to the company's success and which includes a gracious two-story lobby, setting the tone for this high-tech work environment.

ALL PHOTOS BY DOUG HENDERSON

The Hippodrome State Theatre may be known for the challenging and innovative productions it presents during its Mainstage season, but that doesn't mean the company turns its nose up at the classics. In fact, each November and December, loyal theatre enthusiasts look forward to the Hippodrome's outstanding production of *A Christmas Carol*, complete with the kind of acting, whimsical costumes, magnificent sets, and storytelling that transport audiences to another place and time. This type of dedication to the art of theatre makes the rest of the year just as anticipated. Since its founding in 1972 as a startup theatre—the brainchild of artists Bruce Cornwell, Gregory Hausch, Mary Hausch, Kerry McKinney, Marilyn Wall, and Orin Wechsberg—the Hippodrome has produced more than one hundred world, American, and southeastern premieres and become one of Gainesville's most renowned and prolific cultural resources. And when the stage goes dark for the season, the theatre itself does not; it becomes a movie house that screens first-run foreign, limited-release, and avant-garde films.

GAINESVILLE — E*VERY* P*ATH* *starts with* P*ASSION* 105

FloridaWorks: Workforce Solutions for Your Business

FloridaWorks provides convenient workforce solutions for area employers and job seekers through programs that recruit, train, and retain employees. From the first day a business links with FloridaWorks, staff members help employers stay competitive by recruiting and screening applicants, hosting job fairs, and providing information about training grants and opportunities.

> FloridaWorks plays an integral part in Gainesville's economic development.

One of the resources FloridaWorks uses to find and match job seekers with employers is the Employ Florida Marketplace, a comprehensive online database located at www.EmployFlorida.com. Employers can post jobs and access local labor market information, while job seekers can post their résumés, search jobs, and utilize career development tools to enhance their prospects.

FloridaWorks also administers the Florida Ready to Work credentialing program, which measures job skills and work habits. Through this program, candidate credentials can be compared to Equal Employment Opportunity Commission–compliant Florida Ready to Work job profiles to determine which applicants are best suited for the job.

The FloridaWorks Business Services team, based in the Gainesville Area Chamber of Commerce offices, coordinates a variety of services, including employer/employee matching, targeted hiring events, and increased marketing opportunities for open positions. Partnering with the Chamber ensures that Gainesville's workforce continuously grows and improves to meet the needs and opportunities of our community.

From homegrown businesses to national corporations, from startups in Alachua County's incubators to a company's one hundredth anniversary, FloridaWorks plays an integral part in Gainesville's economic development by supporting, training, and growing the area's workforce. ■

FloridaWorks grows businesses and jobs through programs that help businesses connect with skilled workers. The organization's programs focus on recruitment, training, and retention of employees.

BOTH PHOTOS BY GENE BEDNAREK

When running a race with your canine, you'd better try your doggone hardest to be best in show. One of the oldest and most popular of Gainesville's official runs, the 1-Mile Fun Run is part of the Florida Track Club's Annual Dog Days 5K at Gainesville's Westside Park. People and pooches hit the road at 9 a.m. for a lap around the park's perimeter with awards for the zero- to forty-pound winner and the forty-pound-and-over winner. There's no need to whine or howl if you lose the race by a nose, because special prizes are available in other unique categories: Dog and Owner Look-Alike, Slowest Dog, Biggest Dog, and Cutest Dog.

GAINESVILLE — EVERY PATH *starts with* PASSION

Exactech Inc.

Exactech: Joint Replacements That Restore Quality of Life

Exactech began with a conversation at the kitchen table between orthopaedic surgeon Bill Petty, his wife Betty, and biomedical engineer Gary Miller. They founded Exactech in 1985 to make a difference in the lives of people suffering from debilitating joint diseases by developing restorative implants based on input from surgeons.

Twenty-plus years later, Exactech is a publicly traded company with annual revenues in excess of $120 million employing more than three hundred people worldwide. Exactech products include knee, hip, and shoulder systems, as well as spinal products and biologic materials to help people resume active lives.

Exactech's success stems, in part, from its multifaceted approach to product development. "We're constantly looking for new things applicable to joint restoration that could lead to improving a patient's daily activities," says Gary Miller, Ph.D., cofounder and executive vice president of research and development. "We do that through our own research, by attending meetings worldwide, and most importantly, by listening to our surgeon customers who are responsible for implanting these devices and are close to the diseases that we are trying to treat."

Although deciding which products are most viable can be difficult, Miller says Exactech has a unique advantage in the market. "Because of our customer-centric approach to development and our ability to be quite nimble, we're often able to more quickly bring innovative products and instrumentation to the marketplace. This works to our advantage in a rapidly evolving industry."

The Exactech company culture is one where people are passionate about their work, feel empowered to act, and enjoy their

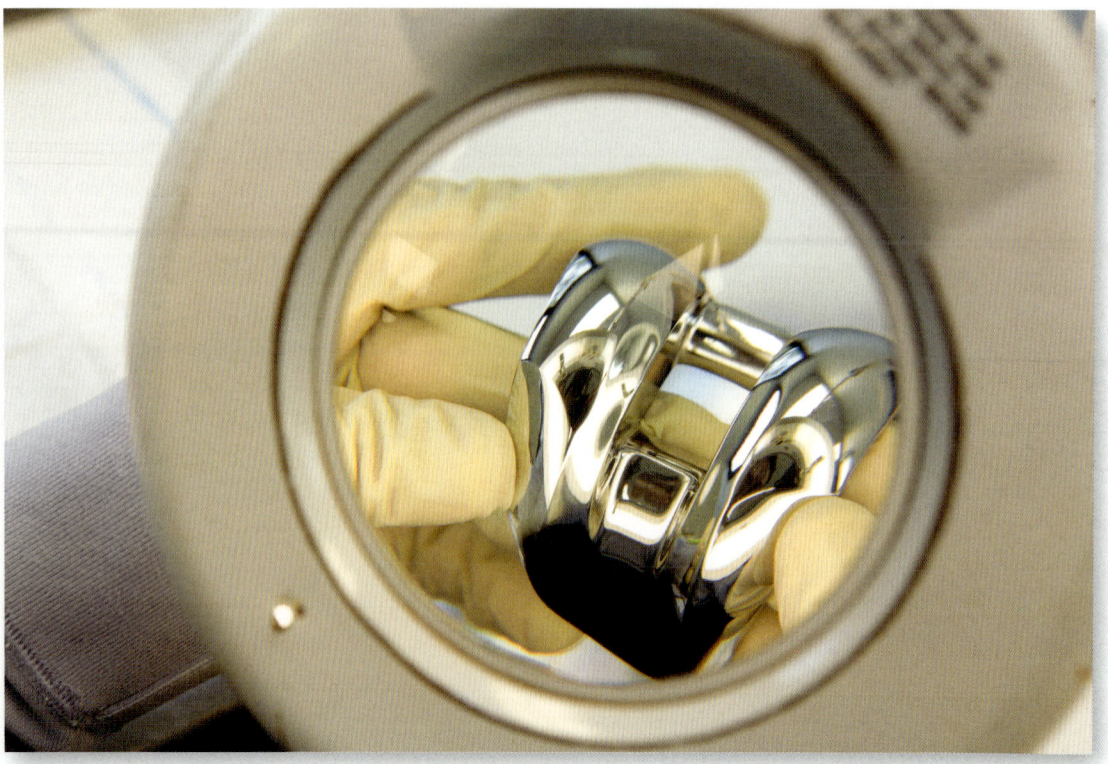

> The Exactech company culture is one where people are passionate about their work.

An Exactech polisher puts the final touches on the Optetrak® knee femoral component by making sure the implant is free from any imperfections.

PHOTO BY SCOTT INDERMAUR

108 GAINESVILLE — EVERY PATH *starts with* PASSION

colleagues professionally and personally. In fact, visitors often comment on the friendliness of employees and their genuine understanding of the company's purpose. Preserving that culture is vital to Exactech, recognized as one of fifteen Top Small Workplaces by *The Wall Street Journal*. "The adage that a company's most valuable resource is its people is absolutely true here at Exactech," says David Petty, president. "In my view, we have the best people in the orthopaedic device industry working here."

With growing numbers of active adults and aging seniors needing care for deteriorating joints, Exactech continues to explore opportunities in earlier intervention, new biological materials, and faster, less painful surgical procedures. "Exactech has had extraordinary success getting to where we are today," says Petty. "But twenty years into it, we feel like we're just getting started. The future is extremely bright for Exactech, as we continue to deliver on our brand promise of making every day 'A Great Day in the O.R.' for the surgeon, the hospital staff, and above all, for the patients we have the privilege to serve." ∎

Exactech Biologics research and development manager Dr. Kurt Sly demonstrates the unique handling properties of Optecure® Phasic™, one of the company's innovative new bone regeneration materials.

GAINESVILLE — EVERY PATH *starts with* PASSION   109

"Let the Gator growl!" This unique pep rally has been a University of Florida homecoming tradition for more than eighty football seasons. Gator Growl is the largest student-produced event of its kind in the world, hosted by Florida Blue Key, a prestigious leadership honorary society. Each year hundreds of Blue Key members merge their brains and brawn to put the event together from drawing board to full stage. The students and community have come to expect clever skits, big-name celebrities, and popular bands to deliver pop culture laughs and music. The introduction of the football team, with special recognition for players who are seniors and participating in their last college homecoming game, tugs a bit at the heartstrings. It's a night to remember, and a guaranteed way to unify the Gator Nation.

ALL PHOTOS BY GENE BEDNAREK

GAINESVILLE — EVERY PATH *starts with* PASSION 111

Fletcher Mortgage Company

Fletcher Mortgage Company—Making Great Places to Live

At Fletcher Mortgage Company, helping clients find the best financing option for their home or commercial property is more than a business matter. "Ours is a more personal approach," says principal Blake Fletcher. "We're dedicated to helping clients find a loan that is right for them, not something that could place them in harm's way."

The preferred lender for Legacy Realty and Properties and area builders, Fletcher Mortgage Company is a full-service brokerage that operates on the belief in going the distance for clients. "If it helps our clients, we're open to it," says Fletcher. "We've found that we can better serve our clients by taking a personal interest in their situation, then using our knowledge of the market to address their specific needs."

Growing relationships with area financial institutions gives Fletcher Mortgage an edge when securing the best financing options, a factor that allows the firm to listen to clients and fit financing specifically to each circumstance. "We look at the entire financial situation," says Fletcher. "It's very important to us to tailor the product to the person's need."

As a result, Fletcher Mortgage is earning a reputation as a customer-centered company. "In the end, customer service is what it's all about," says Fletcher. "People want to work with someone who's knowledgeable and can answer questions, who will take five minutes out of their day to call and update them. The purchase of a home is a big transaction for most people, and we want them to be

> "We're dedicated to helping clients find a loan that is right for them, not something that could place them in harm's way."

Located in the heart of the Gainesville financial district, Fletcher Executive Center offers tenants a distinctive address for their business operations. The three-story, red-brick property is located near three major arteries and is a short distance from Forty-third Street and Newberry Road.

BOTH PHOTOS BY DOUG HENDERSON

knowledgeable as to our every effort on their behalf."

Blake Fletcher is a fourth-generation Gainesville, Floridian, following in the footsteps of a family well-versed in the real estate industry. His father, George E. "Cotton" Fletcher, principal of Legacy Property Development, has led the family team in creating landmark developments like Fletcher Park; Savannah Station; Palm Grove; Countryside Forest, Fletcher Executive Center, the professional home of prominent Gainesville attorney Gloria Fletcher, Blake's mother; and Fletcher's Mill, once the family farm and timber mill. Blake and his sisters are also part of the development entity, and three of the four siblings, including Blake, hold real estate agent licenses, selling homes and other properties as part of the family's real estate company, Legacy Realty and Properties.

In 2007, Blake branched out and formed Fletcher Mortgage Company, accompanied by longtime friend and mortgage industry veteran, Matt Neimark. The mortgage arm rounds out the Fletcher family's offerings and makes buying, selling, or developing real estate as easy as one-stop shopping. Whether it is a home, a commercial building, or a community development, the Fletcher entities can help clients through every detail of the real estate process.

The comprehensive scope of the

(Left to right) Father and son, George E. "Cotton" and Blake Fletcher, at the former Fletcher family farm and timber mill—now the site of Fletcher's Mill, one of the area's landmark residential developments.

Continued on page 114

GAINESVILLE — Every Path *starts with* Passion 113

Fletcher Mortgage Company

ALL PHOTOS BY DOUG HENDERSON

(Left to right) George E. "Cotton" and Blake Fletcher at the entrance to Fletcher's Mill, a Legacy Property Development community. Fletcher Mortgage Company is the preferred lender for Legacy Realty and Properties as well as area builders.

Fletcher Mortgage continued from page 113

Fletchers' services also demonstrates the commitment to the place called home. From first-time homebuyers to flourishing professionals to retirees scaling down, Fletcher developments are geared toward making the area a great place for people to live. "Our developments speak to our family tradition, our heritage," says Blake. "We are a local company that cares about what happens to the land and to the people in our communities. In fact, we take such pride in our own developments that we choose to live and raise our families in them."

Blake Fletcher with his mother, prominent Gainesville attorney Gloria Fletcher. Working with family and friends is one of the perks of his chosen career, says Blake, whose lifelong goal is to continue the legacy of his parents' accomplishments. "I want the Fletcher name to be remembered as one that improves life for others," he says.

Blake Fletcher, principal of Fletcher Mortgage Company, oversees a firm that takes a more personal approach to helping clients with their financing needs: "We've found that we can better serve our clients by taking a personal interest in their situation, then using our knowledge of the market to address their specific needs."

114 GAINESVILLE — EVERY PATH *starts with* PASSION

(Left to right) Matt Neimark, Blake Fletcher, and Cotton Fletcher at the offices of the Fletcher family realty entities. Together, the Fletcher companies make buying, selling, or developing real estate as easy as one-stop shopping.

For Blake Fletcher, a commitment to Gainesville is more than a trait instilled since childhood; it is a lifelong goal. "I enjoy what I do; I work with my family, I work with my best friends. I'm really proud of both my parents and what they've accomplished in their lifetime, and I want to continue the legacy that they began and pass it on to my children and grandchildren. I want the Fletcher name to be remembered as one that improves life for others." ∎

Blake Fletcher (left) branched out and formed Fletcher Mortgage Company, accompanied by longtime friend and mortgage industry veteran Matt Neimark, bringing the Fletcher family's real estate offerings full circle. Whether it is a home, a commercial building, or a community development, the Fletcher entities can help clients through every detail of the real estate process.

GAINESVILLE — EVERY PATH *starts with* PASSION

PHOTO BY ALAN S. WEINER

Getting a good start in life is so important. The midwives and staff at the Birth Center of Gainesville know this all too well, which is why they take such care with the families who come to this facility to experience the most exciting moments of their lives. Located in the fully renovated historic Howard-Kelley House, the Birth Center—which features two birthing suites, a self-standing birthing cottage, a library, and much more—is like a home away from home, allowing new mothers and fathers to feel truly comfortable in their surroundings. They can also feel comfortable knowing that they are bringing their bundles of joy into the world in the oldest birth center on the East Coast.

PHOTO BY ROD REILLY

Mill Creek Farm covers hundreds of acres of serene, tree-studded rolling pastures, and spectacular views. Sounds like a perfect place to retire and it is . . . for horses like Picasso, who came from a riding academy in New York City where he had spent years being used for riding and jumping lessons. Retirement Home for Horses Inc. was created in 1984 by Mary and Peter Gregory to provide a place of peace and tranquility for old, abused, or abandoned horses. This not-for-profit organization depends solely on individual contributions. More than one hundred horses receive individual attention, food, grooming, and veterinary care, not to mention getting a special treat from Mary every once in a while.

GAINESVILLE — E*VERY* P*ATH starts with* P*ASSION*

118 GAINESVILLE — Every Path *starts with* Passion

ALL PHOTOS BY DOUG HENDERSON

Who says there's no such thing as time travel? Visitors to Dudley Farm Historic State Park can go back to the nineteenth century and witness what life on a working Florida farm was like from 1850 to the mid-1940s. Nick Carter works up a sweat cutting firewood, some of which will end up in Audrey Gilstrap's stove. It's no easy trick to keep the oven at just the right temperature so her biscuits turn out perfectly every time. There is always lots of work to be done, and Lee Wiltbank has found a way to use tractor power to help him through his chores. Visitors who linger on the porch can listen to John Catches play banjo and imagine what it would be like to plant crops, tend animals, and get all those other jobs done. In addition to demonstrations, guided tours, and musician guests, the park also has a visitor center, picnic area, and nature trail.

GAINESVILLE — EVERY PATH *starts with* PASSION

North Florida Regional Medical Center

North Florida Regional Medical Center: A Community of Healing

"Working at North Florida Regional Medical Center provides a sense of unity due to the capability, commitment, and quality of doctors and staff."

People tend to feel safe and comfortable in a community setting, and since its founding in 1972, North Florida Regional Medical Center (NFRMC) has formed a close-knit community of medical staff, employees, and patients. "Working at North Florida Regional Medical Center provides a sense of unity due to the capability, commitment, and quality of doctors and staff," says Jamie Thomas, president and CEO.

The center's presence on Newberry Road is a familiar landmark and a visible symbol of its commitment to service.

NFRMC is a full-service medical and surgical acute-care center offering comprehensive heart care, cancer care, women's health, senior care, orthopedics, neurosurgery, and spine services, and it continues to grow to meet the needs of the community. With more than four hundred physicians on staff, representing forty different specialties, patients know they can expect the very best health care and the latest technology available.

North Florida Regional has earned numerous distinctions. It is among an elite few nonteaching hospitals to be recognized eight times as one of the 100 Top Hospitals. Recently, the Center for Obesity Surgery and Treatment has been designated a Center of Excellence for Bariatric Surgery.

"Doctors, nurses, and staff here all put

Having a baby is a special moment for any mother, and at the Women's Center at North Florida Regional, it is the very best experience possible. Recognized as having one of the top-ten maternity units in the nation by *Child* magazine, the Women's Center is there to help with all maternity needs—from pregnancy care to postpartum care, and even parent education. Another convenience is that many obstetricians and pediatricians have their offices on site.

PHOTO BY ALAN S. WEINER

PHOTO BY MIKE SHEA

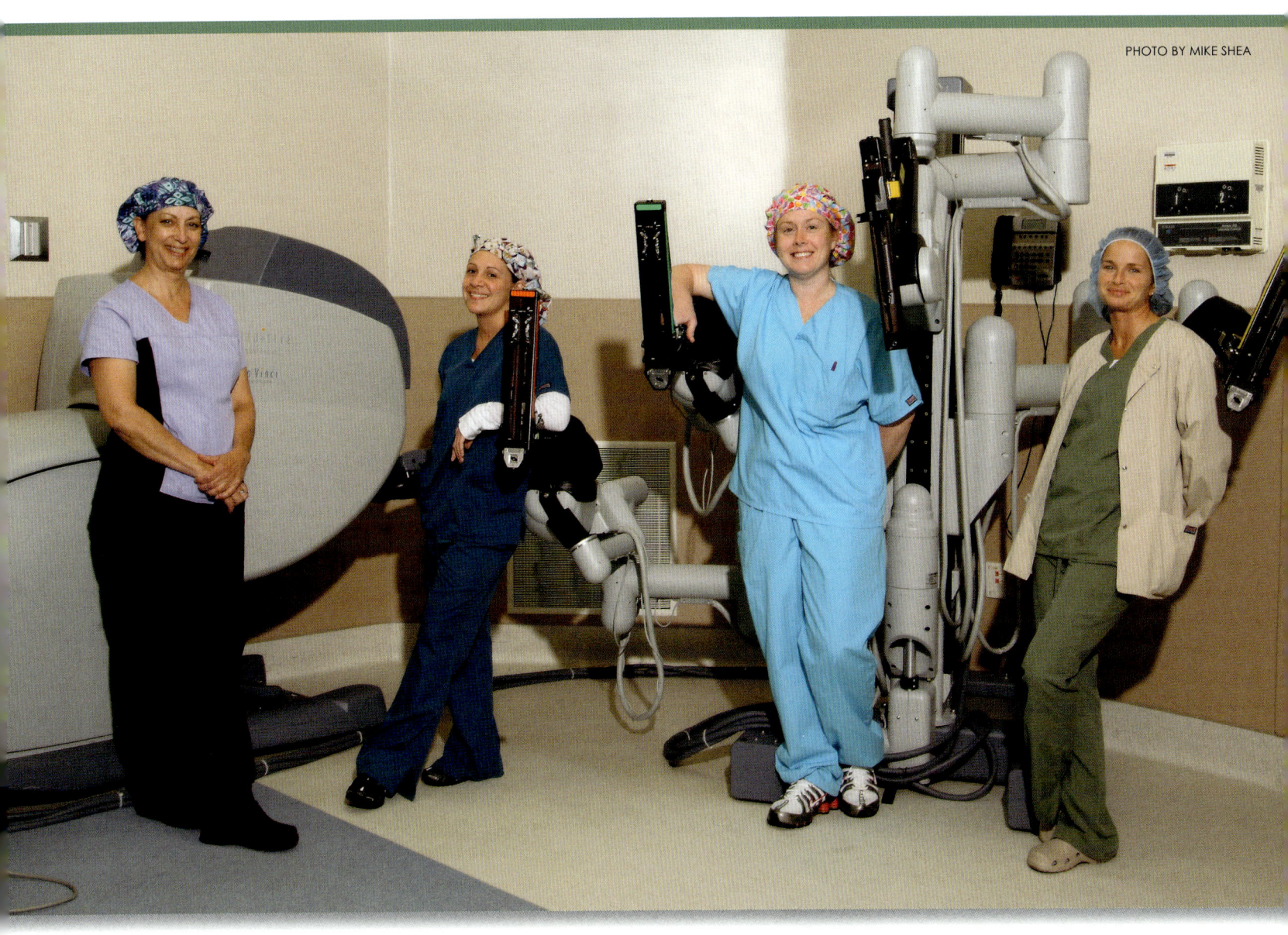

our energy into one simple goal: trying to be better every day than we were the day before," says Marie Johnson, vice president of operations and quality.

North Florida Regional's services incorporate state-of-the-art technologies. Wound Therapy Services has two hyperbaric (HBO) chambers that push 100 percent oxygen to a cellular level that promotes better healing for nonhealing wounds.

Invision, an outpatient imaging center, features a 3T MRI, the only one in the area. In 2008, Invision will introduce the new sixty-four-slice computed tomography (CT) scanner, which has the highest resolution and the fastest imaging times available.

Also at North Florida Regional is CyberKnife® technology, the most advanced radiosurgery system in use today, providing treatment for previously inoperable tumors.

Most recently, NFRMC has implemented the da Vinci® Surgical System, an advanced robotic and computer technology designed to expand the surgeon's capabilities and offer minimally invasive surgery.

NFRMC values the community. The employees and medical staff are leaders in numerous community causes. Hospital employees are a major source of funding for the United Way, recently raising more than $130,000. North Florida Regional annually supports and contributes to many community organizations, including the American Heart Association, Making Strides Against Breast Cancer, and the March of Dimes.

In all, NFRMC is a community within a community, working hard to provide the highest-quality, most cost-effective healthcare services that exceed the needs and expectations of the community it serves. ∎

The da Vinci® Surgical System at North Florida Regional Medical Center provides surgeons with an alternative to both traditional open surgery and conventional laparoscopy. It puts the surgeon's hands at the controls of a state-of-the-art robotic platform, which means they can perform even the most complex and delicate procedures through very small incisions with unmatched precision.

GAINESVILLE — EVERY PATH *starts with* PASSION

The amazing Wall of Wings is a captivating showcase of the world's second-largest collection of Lepidoptera, the species that includes butterflies and moths. The wall is housed in the McGuire Center for Lepidoptera and Biodiversity, part of the Florida Museum of Natural History located on the University of Florida campus. In addition to the wall, the center's features include research laboratories and the three-story Butterfly Rainforest, which immerses visitors in a tropical, colorful, ever-moving world of butterflies.

PHOTO BY ROD REILLY

PHOTO BY ROD REILLY

PHOTO BY ROD REILLY

PHOTO BY DOUG HENDERSON

GAINESVILLE — EVERY PATH *starts with* PASSION 123

Keith Watson Productions

Keith Watson Productions Makes Memorable Events

When Keith Watson Productions is the creative brainpower behind a special event, the affair is sure to be a crowd pleaser—a truly special event. Take Gainesville Harley-Davidson's Chamber of Commerce mixer, for example. With motorcycles on lifts serving as the "centerpieces" atop buffet tables, an Elton John impersonator singing crowd favorites, and lighting to set the "club" mood, the service-department-turned-'70s-retro-disco-nightclub had people mixing and dancing and wishing the evening wouldn't end.

"We custom design each event," says Watson.

"Keith Watson is a highly creative human being. He's one of those people who can take an idea and bring it to life," says Chuck Dalba, marketing director for Gainesville Harley-Davidson. "His energy is off the hook, his staff top-notch. We're fortunate to have the level of expertise Keith provides right here in Gainesville."

Keith Watson Productions is a full-service special-events planning company with an A-list client list that includes prominent businesses and individuals in North Central Florida and New York City. With more than twenty years of experience in the food and

From holiday happenings to serious soirees, Keith Watson Productions makes certain that every affair is unique and memorable.

beverage industry, particularly in the area of special-events planning, Watson has designed and produced events for such notable clients and guests as the University of Florida Alumni Association, the American Heart Association, the Lawton Chiles family, the U.S. Military Academy at West Point, President Bill Clinton, Lady Bird Johnson, and PGA Golf tournaments. His venues are varied as well: from Madison Square Garden to the Boston Opera House, from Callaway Gardens to the Atlanta Botanical Gardens, and from the Metropolitan Museum of Art in New York City to the University of Florida's O'Connell Center.

"We custom design each event," says Watson. "We meet with our clients and talk with them to grasp a sense of their personality, whether that is a corporation or an individual. It's important to understand the purpose of the event, as well as what they want to achieve. We go back with ideas, and without exception, every one of our clients say that we went far beyond their expectations. That's what we take pride in, because after all, you are only as good as your last event."

Watson's clients also say he is easy to work with. "He is so flexible in taking care of what I need," says Penny Jones, who relies on Watson to decorate her home for the holidays. "I think the fact that he was raised on a farm in Alabama makes him easy to work with, but his New York influence allows him to have visions grander than what you might expect," she says. "He blends all of his experiences into a very nice package of high style, but very down to earth." ■

"Attention to detail" is what clients say is the strength of Keith Watson Productions.

ALL PHOTOS BY GENE BEDNAREK

Chef Billie DeNunzio instructs students in decorating techniques as part of classes at Eastside High School's Institute of Culinary Arts. The top-ranked school-to-career program prepares students through training in every aspect of food service and hospitality. From accounting and food safety to nutrition and customer service, students gain knowledge and practical experience before graduation. Their training includes practical application of studies in the onsite eatery, the Hungry Ram Café.

GAINESVILLE — EVERY PATH *starts with* PASSION 127

Meridian Behavioral Healthcare Inc.

Meridian Behavioral Healthcare Replenishes the Community through Recovery

When John Martin was arrested while purchasing drugs, his sentence included mandatory rehabilitation therapy. Heavily addicted to drugs and alcohol, Martin began in-house counseling at Bridge House, one of several residential treatment options offered by Meridian Behavioral Healthcare Inc. As a nonprofit center, Meridian's services have

Based in Gainesville, the center serves the population of eleven counties, having helped seventeen thousand people with a diversity of services in the past year.

evolved over the past thirty-five years, but the organization's vision of a community in which "choice, hope, and recovery are within everyone's reach" has remained the same.

Based in Gainesville, the center serves the population of eleven counties, having helpled seventeen thousand people with a diversity of services including outreach, prevention, rehabilitation, outpatient therapy, residential treatment, substance abuse detoxification, case management, crisis stabilization, and medical outpatient care in the last year alone.

"Mental illnesses affect one in five families in this country, are the second leading cause of premature death and disability, and affect more people than cancer," says Karen Rice, vice president of public relations and development. This reality inspires Meridian's six hundred employees to provide the safety net for a large but often ignored population, reintegrating them into the community as productive citizens.

Martin completed his treatment at Bridge House, graduated from college, and owns and operates several successful businesses with his wife, Kathy, also a Bridge House graduate. In addition, he has served as the mayor of Hawthorne, Florida, is currently its vice mayor, and works as a Meridian counselor.

"When I thought my life was over, it was just beginning," Martin says. "Meridian restores hope." He and his wife have remained sober for nineteen years (and counting). ■

John Martin, a graduate of Meridian Behavioral Healthcare's Bridge House, stands before the facility that changed his life. He credits the staff and counselors at the Gainesville, Florida, location with helping him overcome his substance abuse problems. Now nineteen years sober, he is a successful business owner, has served as mayor and vice mayor of his town, and works as a counselor at Meridian.

PHOTO BY SCOTT INDERMAUR

Alexandra Piriz and Ron Williams walk across the high element, an exciting part of Meridian Behavioral Healthcare's team-building Challenges Ropes Course.

GAINESVILLE — EVERY PATH *starts with* PASSION 129

BOTH PHOTOS BY SCOTT INDERMAUR

Strolling along the one-and-a-half-mile paved walkway that zigzags through the Kanapaha Botanical Gardens is like taking a private tour through Mother Nature's very own backyard. This beautiful sixty-two-acre facility, which is owned and operated by the North Florida Botanical Society, is home to some of the most unique and exclusive collections in the Southeast, offering visitors the chance to see grand and exotic flora from faraway lands, as well as exquisite plants and flowers that are native to Florida. In fact, among the Botanical Gardens' fourteen gardens are the state's largest public display of bamboo, the largest herb garden in the Southeast, a display of giant Victoria water lilies and Asian snake arums, and much more.

ALL PHOTOS BY ALAN S. WEINER

One might not associate Florida with cowboys and cattle, but because of Spanish explorers, such as Ponce de Leon, who began the beef-raising industry there, Florida is America's oldest cattle-raising state. Today, raising cattle remains one of the state's biggest businesses, evidenced by modern-day cattlemen such as Dr. Roger West. West, a retired professor emeritus of the University of Florida with a doctorate in animal science, has operated a commercial cattle ranch in Gainesville for decades, just as his parents did. "When it's profitable, I like the industry a lot," says West of his thousand-acre ranch, which specializes in the sale of calves. During calving season, cowboys Samuel R. Tripson (left) and William R. Butler ride the range to round 'em up, deliver feed, or just troubleshoot in an industry in which no two days are alike. This doesn't bother Tripson, who says of his profession, "I enjoy it very much. It relieves the stress of everything else that goes on."

GAINESVILLE — E*very* P*ath* starts with P*assion*

Infinite Energy

Infinite Energy Offers Infinite Possibilities for Its Employees

Excitement filled the air. Enthusiasm and great anticipation swept through the building as employees cheered for each other's great fortune. As employees approached the stage to receive their prizes from the company's owners, the display of gratitude ranged from shouts of joy and tears to great applause. This describes the atmosphere at the last Infinite Energy Christmas party, where employees won cash prizes ranging from twenty-five hundred to fifty thousand dollars. This also describes the energized working environment and culture at Infinite Energy on any given day.

Owners Darin Cook and Rich Blaser founded Infinite Energy, a natural gas marketing company, in 1994. The philosophy that the owners espouse is that their employees are the company's most valued asset. Because of the employees' creative minds, innovation, and ingenious spirit, Infinite is positioned as an emerging leader within the natural gas industry. Infinite has experienced continued growth since its inception; the employee base has expanded from three to more than three hundred in its Florida, Georgia, New York, and New Jersey offices.

Joy Donaldson, recruiter in human resources, enjoys recruiting top talent for Infinite. "The sound ethics of the owners reign throughout the halls of Infinite. The company really sells itself. I take pleasure in recruiting diverse candidates. The melting pot of cultures, backgrounds, and ingenuity among the employees who work at Infinite

> "The sound ethics of the owners reign throughout the halls of Infinite. The company really sells itself."

Infinite Energy is known for its corporate culture of open communications and ethics.

PHOTO BY DOUG HENDERSON

132 GAINESVILLE — *Every Path starts with Passion*

largely contributes to the company's success. Infinite prides itself on promoting from within, and there are many employees who have been promoted from within the company in a relatively short time."

Jesse Eisner is one of several employees who has risen through the ranks. He started part-time in commercial sales in 1999 while pursuing his degree. Eisner says, "I was hired into the Traderoom immediately following graduation, and I have been promoted twice in the past four years." Eisner is currently the deputy director of the Traderoom and is responsible for buying and selling over $400 million worth of natural gas per year. Lily Shi is another example. She started as a customer service representative in 2004, was promoted three times in less than three years, and is now the Asian market sales manager, responsible for obtaining new customers for Infinite in the Georgia market. Camilo Calvo began in customer service and now manages the regulatory affairs department in the Georgia location. Undeniably, the career possibilities are infinite at Infinite Energy. ∎

This holiday is especially jolly for employees, who are the lucky recipients of a random drawing for cash ranging from twenty-five hundred to fifty thousand dollars.

GAINESVILLE — EVERY PATH *starts with* PASSION

Gainesville's life-science industry cluster is one of the fastest growing in the nation, fostered by programs and facilities designed to encourage research, business startup, and commercialization. Many of these entities are connected to the University of Florida, including the Gainesville Technology Enterprise Center, assisting with tools, training, and infrastructure, and Alachua's Progress Corporate Park, home of the Sid Martin Biotechnology Incubator. In fact, more than forty-five biotechnology, medical device manufacturing, and medical research companies call Alachua County home. Collectively, this sector employs tens of thousands of educated professionals.

BOTH PHOTOS BY GENE BEDNAREK

NovaMin Technology Inc. is on a mission to improve the world's oral health. The company is partnering with oral care manufacturers worldwide to achieve this mission by adding its innovative ingredient to toothpastes and other dental products. This revolutionary additive, which battles tooth decay and other oral health concerns by amplifying the body's own protection and repair mechanisms in the mouth, has had a positive impact on millions since its launch and is sweeping its way around the globe.

PHOTO BY SCOTT INDERMAUR

PHOTO BY DOUG HENDERSON

From applied genetics to implant manufacturing, Gainesville and Alachua County is an area where scientific discovery thrives. Innovation and ideas are welcome here, fostered by programs that encourage entrepreneurial start-ups and by a university whose research activities have placed it at the forefront of invention.

GAINESVILLE — Every Path *starts with* Passion 135

James Moore & Co., P.L.

James Moore & Co., CPAs: Looking beyond the Numbers

For the members and staff of James Moore & Co., P.L. (JM&Co.), there's much more to accounting than crunching numbers. In fact, since James F. Moore founded the firm in 1964, the over one hundred highly skilled professionals who make up the flourishing company have dedicated themselves to providing clients with a full-service experience—one that is client-focused, going beyond the numbers, considering their needs. With offices in Gainesville, Tallahassee, and Daytona Beach, JM&Co. has brought its unique combination of service and expertise to clients throughout Florida.

At the core of JM&Co.'s extensive range of services is the firm's experienced and knowledgeable tax and audit professionals. The former are focused on developing strategies that help clients reduce current and future taxes, which is accomplished through insightful and timely tax return preparation and year-round proactive planning for tax savings. The latter focuses on improving the quality of clients' financial statements by recommending ways to strengthen management controls and increase financial efficiency, security, and overall profitability. For both groups, having a keen understanding of each client's business and goals is the key to providing the exceptional customer service that has become a hallmark of the company. In addition, because firm members strive to stay abreast of changing tax laws and the latest industry advancements, they are able to adapt to meet the varying needs of their clients in an ever-evolving business climate.

What's more, JM&Co. has moved outside of its traditional CPA services to offer business valuations, information systems consulting, and small business accounting. The firm has created a specialized Information Systems Consulting (ISC) staff to provide clients with

Personal attention is provided for each service, along with a genuine passion for helping clients succeed.

Meeting with clients one-on-one gives the members of JM&Co. a better understanding of their unique needs. Here, an onsite visit to one of Perry Construction's many projects allows the key members of the client's accounting team, (left to right) Breck Weingart (Perry Construction), Ken Kurdziel, and Katie Veal (both with James Moore & Co.), to get a firsthand look at the company's exceptional work.

PHOTO BY DOUG HENDERSON

136 GAINESVILLE — EVERY PATH *starts with* PASSION

everything from accounting software evaluation to network design, installation, and support. JM&Co. also has a dedicated small business accounting department that gives clients access to the combined expertise available from a practiced bookkeeper and a licensed CPA when professional services, such as payroll tax reports and general ledger accounting, are required. Personal attention is provided for each service, along with a genuine passion for helping clients succeed.

For the firm, the same philosophy applies to the community-at-large as well. From creating the Strategic Nonprofit Alliance Partnership (SNAP) to support nonprofit organizations, providing software training to industry professionals, and through firm and personal contributions to organizations such as the United Way of North Central Florida and Junior Achievement, two organizations among the fifty organizations supported, JM&Co. shows it is devoted to helping ensure the success of citizens throughout Gainesville and the surrounding areas. It all adds up to the commitment that remains the essence of the firm's foundation: "Never forget, we are here to serve." ∎

Reaching out into the community with such events as the popular TechToberfest is one of JM&Co.'s signature attributes. Here, Roger Reynolds, senior information systems consultant, makes his way into the highly anticipated workshop while several attendees head toward the Microsoft bus after enjoying an informative morning of technology sessions.

GAINESVILLE — EVERY PATH *starts with* PASSION   137

ALL PHOTOS BY ALAN S. WEINER

As the story goes, once each year a magical kingdom materializes in Alachua County. It is the medieval wonderland of Hoggetowne, where chivalrous knights fight for the honor of fair maidens, talented jugglers like Paul Hudert prove they are on the ball, gypsies reveal fortunes, magicians perform unbelievable feats, and musicians serenade guests. Robert Russell and Helen Claudio get in the swing of things tearing into a royal drumstick or two.

138 GAINESVILLE — EVERY PATH *starts with* PASSION

PHOTO BY ROD REILLY

Safety comes first in Gainesville. Just ask the members of the Gainesville Police Department's Traffic Safety Team, who patrol and monitor the city's streets around the clock. The unit is just one of several the Gainesville PD depends upon to keep locals and visitors out of harm's way, from the Joint Aviation and Bicycle units to the K-9 and Mounted units. Of course, these specialty units are part of the bigger picture for the department, which got its start in the early 1900s and has built a reputation over the years for being truly dedicated to the community it calls home.

M.M. Parrish Construction Company: Building A Legacy

For over sixty years, M.M. Parrish Construction Company has been providing commercial construction services in the Gainesville area. Today, the Gainesville-based company has two offices and serves clients throughout Central and North Central Florida.

The company's growth and continued success are rooted in founder Mercer Moorman Parrish Jr.'s belief that a company should exceed its clients' expectations.

"The reason clients continue to rely on us is simple: we treat our clients fairly and are accountable to them. We provide a quality finished product, completed on time, and we stand behind our work," says Mike Walsh, president and eighteen-year veteran of M.M. Parrish Construction Company.

The work of M.M. Parrish Construction Company has had a lasting impact on the landscape of Gainesville. Parrish helped build the University of Florida, including numerous academic buildings and major expansions to Ben Hill Griffin Stadium. Other projects include Saliwanchik, Lloyd and Saliwanchik, a patent attorney's office on Williston Road; the Naylor Publications corporate headquarters; and the Norman H. Lipoff Hall, a Jewish student center on University Avenue.

The impact of M.M. Parrish Construction Company on the community reaches far

"We provide a quality finished product, completed on time, and we stand behind our work."

The three-story corporate headquarters of Saliwanchik, Lloyd and Saliwanchik is a handsome building and a good representation of the commercial projects built by M.M. Parrish Construction Company.

past buildings. The company has a strong and lasting commitment to being good corporate citizens. Part of that citizenship is the firm's involvement in local civic organizations and charities. Many of the company's employees take active roles in these organizations, including board appointments to the Gainesville Area Chamber of Commerce, Rotary Club of Greater Gainesville, and Junior Achievement of Alachua County.

In addition to these associations, M.M. Parrish Construction Company is a regular supporter of numerous local charities, and is the presenting sponsor of the Tri-County Reading Initiative Golf Scramble.

M.M. Parrish Construction Company is grounded in the Gainesville community

Continued on page 142

For the past forty years, M.M. Parrish Construction has been building commercial construction projects throughout North Central Florida. In that time, the company has overseen the construction of numerous high-profile commercial projects, including the fifty-seven-thousand-square-foot, three-story corporate headquarters for Naylor Publications.

GAINESVILLE — EVERY PATH *starts with* PASSION 141

M.M. Parrish Construction Company

M.M. Parrish Construction continued from page 141

and has kept its founder's vision at the forefront of everything the company does. The commercial contractor continues this client-oriented approach, building on the foundation of craftsmanship, integrity, and dependability laid by Mercer Moorman Parrish Jr. over sixty years ago. ∎

Over the years, M.M. Parrish Construction Company has been involved with the construction of numerous religious facilities. One of their more recent projects was the new worship center for the congregation of Grace United Methodist Church on Newberry Road.

The opening of the Tioga Town Center in the fall of 2006 was the culmination of a three-year, design-build collaboration between M.M. Parrish Construction, Ponikvar & Associates and Dibros Corporation. This retail center has become an instant landmark in west Gainesville and is home to numerous businesses.

142 GAINESVILLE — EVERY PATH *starts with* PASSION

Since 1970 when the Gainesville Raceway held its first Gatornationals event, fans have thrilled to year-round events and the best grass-roots drag racing around. The raceway offers everything from half-scale dragsters driven by kids from eight to seventeen, to motorcycles, street cars, purpose-built but amateur dragsters, and professional race cars. The raceway has long been considered one of the fastest tracks on the National Hot Rod Association (NHRA) circuit. Kurt Johnson—whose father Warren Johnson is also on the circuit—clocked a top speed of 207.13 mph on this track recently driving the ACDelco Pro Stock Car. Gainesville Raceway has the distinction of being one of a limited number of tracks to host one of the twenty-four Powerade drag racing touring professional events, such as the NHRA ACDelco Gatornationals.

GAINESVILLE — EVERY PATH *starts with* PASSION 143

PPI Construction Management

PPI Construction Management: The Right Fit

In the construction management field, success is defined by repeat business, and repeat business is defined by the successful delivery of projects. With more than 80 percent of active clients coming from repeat business, PPI Construction Management's record of performance is the cornerstone of the firm's reputation.

"We win work based on a selective qualifications process—by commitment to quality, the expertise of the team, and our history of building relationships based on experience, value, and trust," explains John Carlson, president. "When people have a choice of which firm they want to manage their project, they won't select you again if you haven't delivered. We're proud that we're repeatedly selected."

PPI began in 1993 as a spin-off of Perry Construction, a successful player in the construction industry for forty years. Today, PPI has earned its own reputation as a premier construction management firm in Florida, growing both in volume of business and geographically under the leadership of its principals John Carlson, Breck Weingart, and Domenic Scorpio. With regional offices in Orlando and the Flagler/Palm Coast area, PPI's resume includes educational, health-care, institutional, criminal justice, and government clients covering a region spanning more than twenty-six counties in the state. In Gainesville, PPI projects include skybox additions to the University of Florida's Ben Hill Griffin Stadium; UF's Health Professions, Nursing, and Pharmacy Complex; the expansion and renovation of the Levin College of Law; Oak Hammock at UF; construction of the Alachua County Courthouse; and the Santa Fe Community College Health Science Building.

Since day one, the firm's goals have set

> Since day one, the firm's goals have set PPI apart: to exceed the expectations of clients.

PPI Construction Management is the right fit for each of its projects, such as the Alachua County Courthouse.

144 GAINESVILLE — EVERY PATH *starts with* PASSION

PPI apart: to exceed the expectations of clients, set the standard for business integrity, create a work environment that attracts the best personnel, and maximize value in the interest of the owner's building programs. The goals begin with PPI's culture. "I believe we place a value on people more so than other companies I'm familiar with," says Carlson. "We're very focused on longevity. We bring people into the company that we think will fit our culture and stay with us a long time. We're fair, we provide leading-edge compensation with excellent benefits, and we celebrate milestones as a family would. All that creates an atmosphere of happy and successful people who produce good work."

In addition, the PPI principals and senior officers have an interactive partnership with the clients. "We're big enough to do just about any kind of project, but small enough to have very close contact and involvement with our clients in the process," Carlson explains. "A lot of companies go out there and put the parts and pieces of the building together. But I think it's really the relationship that we have with our clients, and the architects that we work alongside, that account for the real success we have enjoyed." ∎

Headquartered in Gainesville, PPI Construction Management has built a strong reputation for its work in the public and institutional sectors, including higher-education facilities for the University of Florida.

GAINESVILLE — EVERY PATH *starts with* PASSION 145

PHOTO BY ALAN S. WEINER

No idea is too madcap for the creative minds at Cakes by Jenny Wagner & Co. Bakery & Café. Using only the freshest, finest ingredients, Wagner and crew can create the perfect cake for any occasion. Whether it's a wedding, anniversary, birthday, or other special event, a Jenny Cake makes it an affair to remember. Located in historic downtown, Jenny Cakes also serves up pastries, desserts by the slice, and a selection of fine coffees.

PHOTO BY DOUG HENDERSON

The expressive sign that welcomes visitors to Gainesville's Downtown Community Plaza gives a very good indication of what's to be expected on the other side. A charming arts-based venue that's available for concerts, festivals, church gatherings, and more, the plaza is an eclectic meeting space, where music and merriment take center stage year round. And because it also features a picnic and park area, located right at the corner of East University Avenue and SE 1st Street, it's the perfect gathering spot for people of all ages who want to enjoy the beauty that can be found in the heart of historic Gainesville.

146 GAINESVILLE — EVERY PATH *starts with* PASSION

PHOTO BY DOUG HENDERSON

PHOTO BY DOUG HENDERSON

In addition to its shopping options, the Tioga Town Center often plays host to events of every shape and size. One of the more festive of these was a gala known as A Season of Miracles. The fund-raiser, which was presented by the Davis and Judi Rembert Family Foundation on behalf of the Children's Miracle Network and Shands Children's Hospitals, raised thirteen thousand dollars in 2007, its inaugural year. Guests were treated to an evening of holiday lights, delicious food, jazz entertainment, and horse and carriage rides.

(Left to right) Annie Morton, Margaret Friend, and Lee-Ann Humerik were some of the guests taking part in the evening's activities, which included sparkling holiday decor, delicious food, jazz entertainment, and horse and carriage rides. Guests also bid on a wide variety of items in a silent auction, with the proceeds contributing to the event's efforts to help children in need.

GAINESVILLE — EVERY PATH *starts with* PASSION

Tioga Realty

Tioga Realty: Where Passion Makes the Difference

When it comes to buying and selling property, the emotional investment can be as significant as the financial side of the transaction. The professionals at Tioga Realty not only understand the intricate matters behind real estate endeavors, but they also take a personal interest in making sure clients are secure in their decisions.

"For us, it's not about company volume, it's about the impact we have on our clients' lives," explains Broker Deborah Minck, who guides Tioga Realty's team of associates. "We're more concerned about our clients' overall goals; therefore, we use a unique blend of expertise, experience, and compassion to help them meet their financial objectives."

To really understand each client's goal, Tioga Realty associates delve into matters by probing for hidden answers. "Real estate can be extremely complicated, so we ask pertinent questions, explore needs, and help navigate through the overwhelming amounts of information. This allows the client to make decisions based off the present, as well as the future," says Minck. "We understand the magnitude of the decisions people are making, not just about a single transaction, but how the transaction affects their entire financial portfolio."

In turn, Tioga Realty has earned the loyalty of a host of clients and receives a steady flow of referrals and repeat business. "We want clients for a lifetime, not just for a fleeting transaction," explains Minck. "That's why we work hard to bond with our clients, and we trust that we'll be rewarded in the end when the job is done with a spirit of excellence."

Started as an onsite agency to manage marketing and sales for the distinctive Town of Tioga community, and later additional

> "We want clients for a lifetime, not just for a fleeting transaction."

Absolute convenience for home buyers and sellers is a hallmark of Tioga Realty, as evidenced by its main administration and sales building, located in the heart of Tioga Town Center on West Newberry Road.

BOTH PHOTOS BY SCOTT INDERMAUR

developments, Tioga Realty's focus extends far beyond its original intent. "The Town of Tioga community provides Tioga Realty with the foundation of success and has launched the growing organization into a full-service, multifaceted real estate company," says Town of Tioga developer Luis Diaz.

Whether buying a first home, building a custom home, locating a business, or looking for land to develop, Tioga Realty associates have the expertise to assist with any real estate transaction. "The diversity of our associates matches the diversity of the products we sell. We work together, as a team, to deliver beyond the ordinary for clients," says Greta Rice, sales manager. Tioga Realty's associates' connections also benefit clients who are looking for second homes or expanded business ventures beyond the Gainesville area.

Mirroring their dedication to the industry, Tioga Realty associates also spread their zeal for life through involvement in a wide variety of endeavors that benefit multiple segments of the community. "Strong, benevolent individuals create competent, service-oriented professionals," states Minck. "That is what brings me the most pride—working with quality individuals." Together, Tioga Realty represents a team whose passion for a job well done is truly in helping others succeed. ∎

The Tioga Realty Team of BROKER & REALTOR-Associates includes (from top left) Don Winter, Rick Hammond, Tom Reilly, and Steve Schaff; (middle row) Leah Winter, sales manager Greta Rice, Tricia Reilly, and Pat Schaff; and (front) director of sales and marketing Deborah Minck.

GAINESVILLE — EVERY PATH *starts with* PASSION

From miniatures to wall-sized works, Eleanor Blair captures the vibrant colors and textures of Florida. She works primarily in oil on canvas, but also exhibits works in watercolors, acrylics, and pastels. "I search for beauty in the natural world and the everyday things I see." She moved to Florida in 1971 and is a well-known member of the local art community. Gainesville's picturesque neighborhoods provide not only a sense of tranquility, but also ample inspiration for her city scenes.

ALL PHOTOS BY SCOTT INDERMAUR

John Tilton may practice one of the oldest crafts in the world, but his work is far from dated or old-fashioned. In fact, the porcelain art pottery created by this visionary artist is as contemporary as it is steeped in tradition. The extraordinary bowls, vases, and covered jars he forms by hand in his Alachua studio feature unique yet organic shapes, subtle yet striking colors, and a passion for the art that shines through effortlessly. With a master's degree in mathematics and an M.F.A. in ceramics from the University of Florida, Tilton acknowledges that his masterpieces evolve, going through several stages—and often many months—before being completed. In the end, they are finished with crystalline matte glazes.

Few symbols are more recognizable around the world than the black and red Harley-Davidson logo. In Gainesville it is proudly displayed by the Lytle family on their twenty-five-thousand-square-foot Gainesville Harley-Davidson & Buell showroom. This is a far cry from Harley's humble beginning in 1903, when the company was housed in a ten-by-fifteen-foot wooden shed with its name scrawled on the door.

PHOTO BY GENE BEDNAREK

If you live near Skate Station Funworks in Gainesville, Florida, you don't have to worry about your kids becoming couch potatoes during summer vacation. Several years ago, this thirty-thousand-square-foot family entertainment facility offered a Mad Science Camp for after-school, birthday, and summer entertainment. Not only did the kids like the camp, they also enjoyed the roller skating, rock climbing, miniature golf, batting cages, and go-carts. Science Camp also inspired another summer agenda, Action Camp. "If your children complain that child care is boring, we certainly alleviate that problem because they love it here," says Dave Balogh, general manager.

PHOTO BY ROD REILLY

GAINESVILLE — Every Path *starts* with Passion 151

SantaFe HealthCare Inc. / AvMed Health Plans

SantaFe HealthCare: A Family of Companies That Promotes Healthy Living

SantaFe HealthCare remains dedicated to providing health care and vital services that enhance the quality and dignity of life.

Helping people enjoy life's many stages is the predominant goal of SantaFe HealthCare Inc., the holding company for a family of community-based, not-for-profit organizations that serve Floridians. As a result of focused dedication to that goal, SantaFe HealthCare, based in Gainesville, consistently ranks as a national leader in quality and customer satisfaction for the exemplary service provided through its affiliates: AvMed Health Plans, Haven Hospice, North Florida Retirement Village, and Bayview Gardens.

"Each SantaFe HealthCare affiliate actively collaborates to fulfill the vision of its parent company," says Michael Gallagher, SantaFe president and CEO. "All of the entities are committed to providing health care and vital services that enhance the quality and dignity of life."

Originally established in 1969 as a health plan for the airline industry in South Florida, AvMed Health Plans has since evolved into one of the largest not-for-profit health plans in the state, serving some 250,000 Floridians. Headquartered in Miami, AvMed also has a strong presence in Gainesville and operates four other regional offices, offering a variety of health plan options to small and large employers and Medicare Advantage beneficiaries in South Florida.

The motto of "a health plan with your health in mind" reflects AvMed's determination to cater to the individual with an emphasis on proactive health by offering

Dori Pereyra, nurse coordinator, provides the friendly and helpful service to a patient that makes AvMed's Nurse On-Call process so successful.

PHOTO BY GENE BEDNAREK

programs designed to help members live healthy and productive lives. For example, AvMed's Healthy Expectations program offers incentives for mothers to seek pre- and postnatal care for themselves and their infants (parents are rewarded for bringing in their children for timely immunizations), and the Weight Watcher's reimbursement program adds even more incentive to gain healthy habits. While AvMed's Wellness programs seek to prevent members from suffering with avoidable health conditions, the organization is also focused on supporting and caring for those with chronic conditions who require ongoing intensive and complex care.

SantaFe also operates the retirement communities of North Florida Retirement Village (the Village) in Gainesville, and Bayview Gardens (Bella Terra) in Clearwater. The Village has a beautiful 104-acre campus—filled with small ponds, tall pines, and carefully preserved wetlands and native live oaks—that serves more than

Continued on page 154

The North Florida Retirement Village (the Village), operated by SantaFe HealthCare, serves as a relaxing 106-acre residence for over 460 seniors. The Gainesville region's balmy weather and tropical atmosphere provide the perfect environment for a full range of senior living choices—from independent living apartments and cottages to assisted-living congregate care facilities.

SantaFe HealthCare Inc. / AvMed Health Plans

SantaFe HealthCare continued from page 153

450 seniors. This premier upscale rental retirement community offers various independent-living options, including neighborhood cottage homes, resort-style apartments, assisted living, and a separate residence dedicated to memory support. Likewise, Bayview Gardens offers over 250 residents options that include independent-living rental cottages and assisted-living studio apartments located on thirty-two acres on Tampa Bay.

SantaFe's Haven Hospice provides compassionate care and support for those with life-limiting illness and loss. One of the top twenty hospice and palliative-care programs in the country, Haven Hospice is the largest rural hospice in the United States, serving an average of 650 patients and families daily throughout North Florida, from the Gulf Coast to Jacksonville.

From the promotion and support of healthy lifestyles for all ages, to creating the best of senior living throughout Florida, to providing compassionate hospice and palliative care, SantaFe HealthCare remains dedicated to providing health care and vital services that enhance the quality and dignity of life. ■

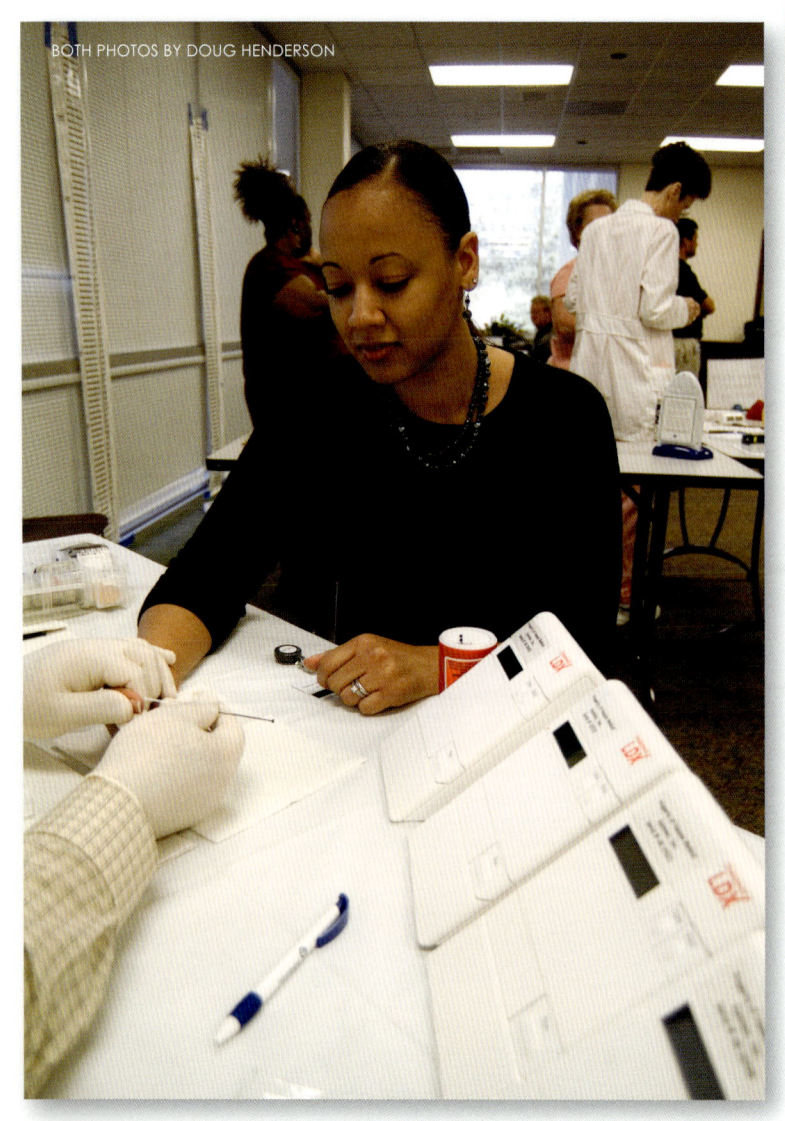

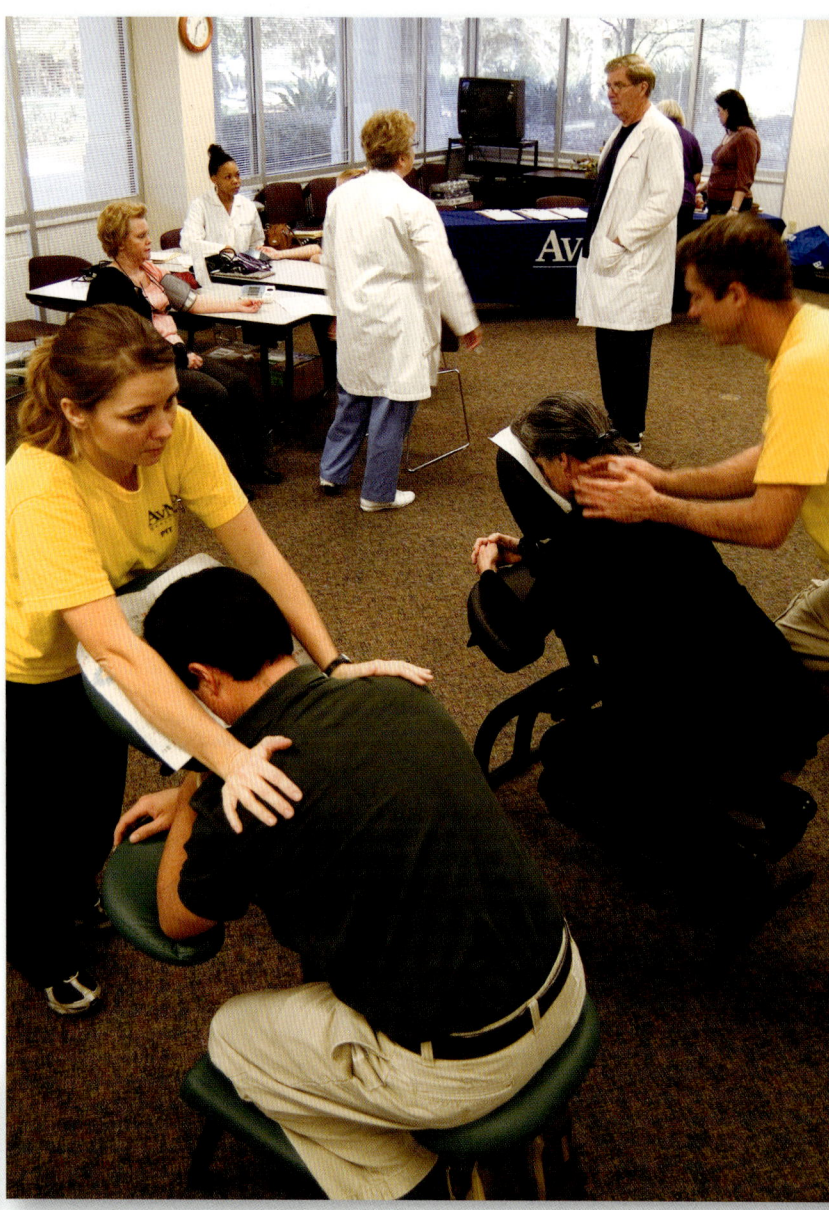

AvMed Health Plan's health fair attracts quite a few participants, including Jennifer Derby, who is undergoing a cholesterol screening.

Proper T. Gator stands proudly in front of Bosshardt Realty's headquarters in Waterford Park. Proper T. was the creation of the Bosshardt marketing department to represent the company's strong market presence in the University of Florida's hometown. Proper T. stands ready to sell real estate with an aura of professionalism. And why not? He attended Bosshardt University's ten-day training course to become a practicing Realtor with Bosshardt.

PHOTO BY SCOTT INDERMAUR

Haven Hospice

Haven Hospice:
Enhancing Life through Our Compassion and Care

Haven Hospice serves sixteen counties in North Florida and provides comprehensive, compassionate care while respecting each person's needs, beliefs, or wishes. Its staff and volunteers live in the communities they serve and are available to Haven's patients and families within two hours of any need.

The organization offers timely responsiveness and access to care; full-time physicians who make house calls; frequent staff visits; full-time pharmacists; home health aides who assist with personal care; aggressive pain and symptom management; and inpatient and respite care, as well as services provided regardless of ability to pay. Haven Hospice also provides caregiver education and support, children's services, and bereavement services before and after death or loss.

Care is provided wherever a patient calls home.

Keeping patients and families in control of their situation by offering options and respecting the choices they make is another Haven Hospice priority. Care is provided wherever a patient calls home—whether it is in an assisted-living facility, a nursing home, a hospital, an apartment, a house, a trailer, or a car.

Haven Hospice also has four inpatient care centers strategically located within its service area that provide a home-away-from-home option for caregivers needing a break from the daily challenges of caring for an ailing loved one, or a patient needing help managing acute pain and symptoms.

The staff and volunteers of Haven Hospice are committed to enhancing life through their compassion and care. Haven Hospice has been serving North Florida since 1979 and has been licensed as a not-for-profit hospice since 1980. ∎

Haven Hospice staff is dedicated to the comfort and the spiritual and emotional well-being of its patients and their loved ones. Pictured here is one of Haven's memorial walkways and gardens.

156 GAINESVILLE — Every Path starts with Passion

PHOTO BY DOUG HENDERSON

Ben Hill Griffin Stadium at Florida Field may be the most well-known "Swamp" in North Central Florida, but it's not the only swamp in Alachua County. The natural diversity throughout the area includes several marshy areas that are perfect for an afternoon airboat ride. Skipping across the top of the water is an exhilarating way to explore the expansive locales that surround the city of Gainesville, including Orange Lake and Lake Lochloosa.

Marriott Residence Inn

Marriott Residence Inn: A Passion for Hospitality

To stay at Marriott Residence Inn is to be surrounded by the comforts of home in a place where people are passionate about making every guest feel welcome.

When guests arrive at the Marriott Residence Inn, they enter a place that immediately evokes a sense of homelike comfort. From a warming lobby hearth to an inviting welcome by the hotel staff—professionals who are eager to ensure a pleasant stay—guests are made immediately to feel safe and comfortable in their surroundings.

A two-story property, the Marriott Residence Inn offers sixty studio suites, each with a separate bedroom, a kitchen, and space furnished for work or dining. Penthouse suites are also available and come complete with extras like loft sleeping accommodations.

Suite accommodations at the Marriott Residence Inn provide for every comfort, with luxurious bedding that includes crisp linens, plump pillows, and thick mattresses. Penthouse bathrooms also offer the little extras—with bathtub spray jets, separate tub and shower, and hair dryers.

Cable channels, color televisions, and fireplaces are other in-room amenities enjoyed by guests in every suite.

For the business traveler, the Marriott offers copy and fax services as well as in-room, high-speed Internet access and wireless connections. Extended-stay services also include valet dry cleaning services and onsite laundry facilities, and for those items needing extra security, safe deposit boxes are available.

Kitchens at the Marriott Residence Inn

> **S**uite accommodations at the Marriott Residence Inn provide for every comfort.

The Residence Inn offers guests a feeling of homelike comfort and safety, with a welcoming staff, eighty suites with private entrances, and all the amenities needed for any length of stay.

158 GAINESVILLE — EVERY PATH *starts with* PASSION

come complete with all the amenities needed to cook a meal, from oven and microwave to refrigerator and dishwasher to cookware and dishes. Not in the mood to cook? The hotel also offers a complimentary buffet breakfast as well as an evening social hour, Monday through Thursday, and dozens of nearby restaurants are ready to deliver. If you enjoy home cooking but are just too busy to go to the market, the hotel offers a grocery shopping service. Feel more like a cookout or picnic? The hotel offers facilities for outdoor entertaining.

If a little recreation is in order, the hotel offers an exercise room as well as an outdoor pool and Jacuzzi.

Stays at the Marriott Residence Inn are eligible for Marriott Rewards Points, one of the world's premier travel award programs.

Located within easy access to area businesses, highways, airports, and attractions, the Marriott Residence Inn is the perfect place for any stay. ■

The hotel's outdoor swimming pool is the perfect place to relax and unwind during the warm summer months. Outdoor amenities also include a sports court and picnic area.

GAINESVILLE — Every Path *starts with* Passion 159

The faculty at the Stephen Foster Academy of Math, Science, and Technology (home of the Steamers) believe in hands-on learning. Working individually and in teams, the third-, fourth-, and fifth-graders participate in sessions that challenge them to higher-order thinking through science and math explorations. With projects such as applying the scientific method to track the growth pattern of their own plants, students such as Hamod McNutt (left) and Jacob Carter, pictured here with Emma Brady, teacher, are well on their way to discovering the link between theory and practice. In the classroom, students Hannah Hill, David Richardson, and Chrystal Merry (above, left to right) prepare to create some steam of their own in that age-old and beloved science project: the volcano.

BOTH PHOTOS BY SCOTT INDERMAUR

160 GAINESVILLE — EVERY PATH *starts with* PASSION

"It's more than a camp; it's an educational adventure!" That slogan perfectly sums up Techno Building Camp. Kids work in a state-of-the-art lab to build real things on a model scale. Campers may register for one of two sessions for design-build projects. In Dream Builders, they select a blueprint and use real tools and materials to build a model house. Computers help in construction, interior design, and assembling miniature furniture. In Toys "N" Things, students build a working model of a toy or amusement park ride. Then they form a company, develop logos, and use computer software, digital cameras, and video production to advertise their products.

PHOTO BY GENE BEDNAREK

GAINESVILLE — Every Path *starts with* Passion   161

Charles Perry Construction

Charles Perry Construction: Building on the Basics

Back in 1968, when Charles Perry started his construction firm, he approached each project with a few standard rules, basics that became the foundation on which one of Florida's leading construction firms was built.

"Chuck's teachings were simple," says Breck Weingart, president, who now co-owns Charles Perry Construction with Brian Leslie, vice president of operations. "Be honest. Do good work. Do it on time. Don't make excuses. In short, you do things the right way all the time, and you can build a pretty good reputation."

Started out of a pickup and trailer, Perry Construction is now a multimillion-dollar operation with offices in Gainesville and Orlando. Its growth is derived, in part, from being open to new opportunities and rarely turning down work as long as resources are available to ensure a quality outcome. "Whether it is a ten-thousand-dollar or $100 million project, if we have the proper team, we will pursue it," explains Weingart. "We are truly committed to meeting or exceeding our customer's needs and expectations."

From offices to operating rooms, parking lots to laboratories, stadiums to classrooms, Charles Perry Construction projects run the gamut of industries and have earned the

"We are truly committed to meeting or exceeding our customer's needs and expectations."

PHOTO BY DAVID JOHNSTON

(Left to right) Breck Weingart, president, and Brian Leslie, vice president of operations, co-owners of Charles Perry Construction, continue to uphold the founder's beliefs: be honest, do good work, do it on time, and don't make excuses.

162 GAINESVILLE — EVERY PATH *starts with* PASSION

company considerable repeat business from clients like the University of Florida, Santa Fe Community College, HCA, Santa Fe Health Care, and Shands Healthcare.

Building such a comprehensive portfolio takes a culture of teamwork, stemming from the founder's belief in trusting in the expertise of others and treating employees like family. As a result, the Perry crew is more than one hundred strong and includes many individuals touting an excess of twenty-five years with the company. Working alongside them to ensure projects are completed to specifications, on time, and within budget are select subcontractors with whom the company has built solid relationships over time.

Perry Construction also makes community betterment its business and is involved in a wide range of organizations. "We have been part of this community for a long time, and we support it in every way we can because that is the right thing to do," says Weingart. "It gives us a great deal of satisfaction to be part of the success in our community."

In honor of its founder, the company takes special interest in supporting programs to train the next generation of trades. As a result, the local apprenticeship program is growing, the community has a high school dual enrollment program, and programs at the University of Florida are enhanced by an adjacent demonstration area and outdoor teaching amphitheater. Through activities like these, Charles Perry Construction ensures a legacy of honesty and integrity that will be creating the landscapes of tomorrow. ■

At North Florida Regional Medical Center, Perry Construction renovated approximately 55,000 square feet of the existing interior and built a four-story, 136,000-square-foot addition to the structure. First-floor features in the new addition include expansion of the lobby and the central sterile supply suite.

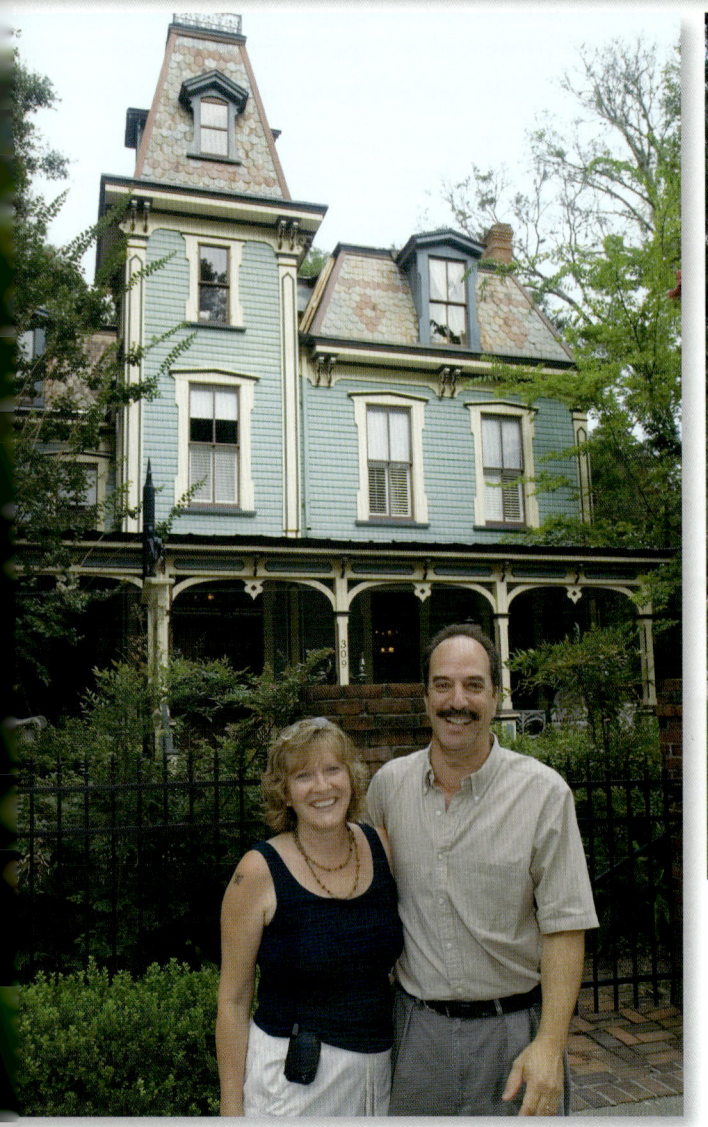

ALL PHOTOS BY ROD REILLY

Steeped in history, yet brimming with modern amenities, Gainesville is the perfect place to experience a bed-and-breakfast. Guests of the area's homelike inns are greeted by friendly folks who know what southern hospitality is all about. Perfectly complementing Gainesville's sleepy, small-town feel, the city's bed-and-breakfasts offer visitors a chance to relax on the porch, stroll through gardens, dine outdoors, peruse local shops, or enjoy an easy night of entertainment.

PHOTO BY ROD REILLY

PHOTO BY DOUG HENDERSON

PHOTO BY DOUG HENDERSON

PHOTO BY ROD REILLY

GAINESVILLE — EVERY PATH *starts with* PASSION   165

Gainesville Health & Fitness Center

Gainesville Health & Fitness Center:
Keeping Gainesville the Healthiest Community in America, One Person and One Business at a Time

Gainesville Health & Fitness Center's name says it all. Far more than the mainstream health club, the award-winning fitness center has been in the business of keeping Gainesville healthy for more than thirty years. In fact, the Gainesville Health & Fitness Center (GHFC) is credited with spearheading the community-wide wellness effort that resulted in Gainesville's coveted designation as the first and only Gold Well City USA from the Wellness Councils of America.

GHFC's being a wellness home, a fitness partner, and a health resource for individuals and businesses alike is a source of pride for owner Joe Cirulli.

"Fitness really has been my whole life. It's who I am, not just what I do," he says. "The business is the connection of two passions: working out and helping people become better than what they are today." Always a man driven by goals, when Cirulli began GHFC in 1976, he did so with one goal in mind: to be one of the best companies for the world. With a focus on honest business practices, talented staff, and an overall belief that everyone should be exercising, Cirulli has accomplished much, including inspiring thousands of people to truly understand the meaning behind the phrase, "If you have your health, you have everything."

Now that Gainesville is a designated Well City, the GHFC team says the current mission is to keep Gainesville the healthiest

"We find ways to help people stay healthy, one person, one company, and one day at a time."

Yoga is one of the many classes that GHFC offers in its Fitness Center for Women.

BOTH PHOTOS BY GENE BEDNAREK

166 GAINESVILLE — EVERY PATH starts with PASSION

community in America. "Businesses know that we are their wellness partner to help employees get and stay healthy," explains Debbie Lee, GHFC's community and worksite wellness director. "That's simply our business, our expertise. The workplace knows the importance of wellness, but they don't always know how to execute the programs, and that's where we step in—as a resource coordinator."

Approaching the process as a partner, GHFC first looks at the needs of the business. If it's information, GHFC can provide speakers on a wide range of topics, from nutrition to stress management. Sometimes employers just need creative ways to engage their employees. North Florida Regional Medical Center is one of the area businesses that participated in the Amazing Race of Fitness, a twenty-one-day team-oriented program to get people moving. "In health-care professions, people put so much emphasis on taking care of others. They need to look after themselves so they

Continued on page 168

"Gainesville Health & Fitness Center is not only a health club and a health resource in our community, as a major employer it has set the tone for the culture of Gainesville—a very fit city," says Tracy Tompkins, project manager for Naylor, LLC, a company with a long-standing relationship with GHFC.

Gainesville Health & Fitness Center

BOTH PHOTOS BY GENE BEDNAREK

GHFC continued from page 167

can be at their best," says Angie Hindle, employee health nurse for North Florida Regional Medical Center. "Typically, those who sign up for the race aren't in an active lifestyle. On top of getting people out to make a change, it ignites the spirit of competition, and every year it has generated many fitness converts," she adds.

That's what Cirulli has known all along: that all of us look for ways to improve. "Most clubs focus on corporate memberships," says Cirulli. "Instead, we find ways to help people stay healthy, one person, one company, and one day at a time." ■

GHFC's goal is to keep Gainesville one of the healthiest communities in America.

There are many ways to engage in fitness activities at GHFC. Some people prefer team sports like basketball, while others pursue an individual workout.

168 GAINESVILLE — EVERY PATH *starts with* PASSION

While its extended hours have made Florida Citizens Bank known area-wide as the "7 to 7 Community Bank," this service is just one of many that the bank has tailored to meet the unique needs of its customers. For individual customers, the bank offers home banking and bill pay, personal checking and loans, and even a debit-card program for people with less-than-perfect credit while commercial customers appreciate unique conveniences like daily spreadsheet e-mails, electronic deposit system, corporate credit cards with instant credit increases and expenditure breakdowns, and an armored car service.

PHOTO BY GENE BEDNAREK

William W. "Billy" Brame, AIA, of Brame Architects, at the Archer Community Center in Archer, Florida, where a remodeling project is turning a 1930s school gymnasium into a community center for everyone to enjoy. Transformation of the structure has been a community-based effort, with various grants and donations from public and private resources helping to turn this significant landmark into a place for meetings, performances, recreation, and more.

PHOTO BY SCOTT INDERMAUR

GAINESVILLE — EVERY PATH *starts with* PASSION   169

BOTH PHOTOS BY ROD REILLY

If the early bird gets the worm, then the early risers in Gainesville get the best produce. That's because they know to make their way to the Alachua County Farmers Market, where they not only can find the freshest and most delicious fruits, vegetables, and herbs around, but also have a delightful conversation with the people who grew those delectable items. Open every Saturday year-round from 8:30 a.m. to 1:00 p.m., the Farmers Market is one of the hottest spots in Gainesville. And during the spring and fall peak growing seasons, when farmers can show off their finest produce, plants, and other agricultural products of the year, a satellite market brings the excitement to Butler Plaza as well.

PHOTO BY ROD REILLY

When Gainesville residents are looking for green products for their homes, all they have to do is take 441 South to Micanopy, the small town that is home to the Mosswood Farm Store, owned and operated by the mother-and-daughter team of Morgan Pevonka and Emily Piazza. The shop, which resides in a charming farmhouse on Cholokka Boulevard, is filled with rooms of organic products, from candles to soaps to food items. In addition, the store features recycled, earth-friendly, and highly unique products, including bicycle-churned ice cream machines, butter churns, solar ovens, and more. They are the type of sustainable goods that not only allow customers to live a truly healthy lifestyle, but that also hearken back to days gone by. And with more people starting to participate in the green movement that's sweeping the country, Mosswood Farm Store is sure to be seen as one of Alachua County's greatest resources.

GAINESVILLE — EVERY PATH starts with PASSION 171

ERA Trend Realty

ERA Trend Realty: Real Estate as Easy as One - Two - Three

Buying or selling a home can be complicated. But deciding to hire ERA Trend Realty is as easy as one-two-three.

One: You want a REALTOR® that has a history in the area, and Trend Realty has been operating in the Gainesville market since 1974.

Two: You want a firm whose associates are trained to focus on your needs and constantly improve their skills to give you the best service possible.

Three: You want a firm with roots in the community whose associates are involved in making it a better place to live and work.

"We're proud to meet all these requirements," said Thomas McIntosh, president of ERA Trend Realty. "The real estate business is always changing, and our strength is that we anticipate trends and stay on top of changes. This gives us an edge that can only come from experience, from being in business long enough to be able to interpret trends, and not having to rely on hype or outside information."

Trend Realty has an ever-expanding sales force that constantly undergoes in-house

"*Consistently customers tell us they would hire us again, and they would recommend us to their friends and family.*"

Jan Baur, vice president of ERA Trend Realty, and Michael Blachly, director of the Phillips Center, discuss upcoming performances at the Phillips Center.

PHOTO BY DOUG HENDERSON

training. "Tony Miller, our sales manager, has been with us since 1982," said McIntosh. "He takes the lead on training, but all our management team is involved because each one has something unique to impart to our associates. We have an extensive training program for new hires, but all our associates take part in ongoing training.

"We have very high expectations for our customer service, and one of the ways we ensure this is to have an independent firm survey each of our customers, both buyers and sellers. Consistently customers tell us they would hire us again, and they would recommend us to their friends and family. That's our ultimate criteria."

When it comes to being involved in the community, Trend Realty has an equally outstanding reputation. Its support for charities is across the board, and Trend's associates are truly a part of the community, supporting many groups with time, talent, and financial donations.

In recent years the firm has focused support on the University of Florida's Cultural Plaza, which includes the Phillips Center for the Performing Arts, the Florida Museum of Natural History, and the Harn Museum of Art. Gainesville values those organizations, which increase the quality of life.

"We are fortunate to have the UF Cultural Plaza in Gainesville. It is the crown jewel of our community and the cultural center of North Central Florida," said McIntosh.

One-two-three: history, training, community. That's Trend Realty. ■

Rebecca Martin Nagy, director of the Harn Museum of Art, and Tommy McIntosh, president of ERA Trend Realty and a sponsor of the museum, both appreciate the significance of the Harn and the contribution it makes to Gainesville's quality of life. One of the highlights of the museum's holding of European art includes French Impressionist painter Claude Monet's landscape *Champ d'avoine*. Painted in 1890, it depicts a scene in the vicinity of Giverny, the French village where the Monet family lived.

Professionals Title Company: Making Houses into Homes℠

When the best professionals and the best systems combine for title and settlement services, the result is a seamless transaction and satisfied customers. Professionals Title Company is that kind of company, with a track record for results.

"From my experience, real estate closings can be hectic and emotional, creating a lot of anxiety for both buyers and sellers," explains Walt Mullen, a principal of Professionals Title Company. "When our customers sit down at the closing table, the transaction is smooth, not only because our professional staff are highly trained experts, but also because the people behind the scenes have the expertise and the necessary systems to ensure a smooth settlement." Professionals is a member of the Title Resource Group family of companies (TRG) —a driving force in the national title and settlement industry. Consequently, Professionals can provide exceptional service that is national in scope, yet local in nature, and focused on solution-oriented communication for all parties involved. An affiliation with ERA Trend Realty strengthens the team's understanding of the local real estate customs, requirements, and regulations and makes Professionals Title Company an active member of the Gainesville business community.

Simply put, Professionals Title Company is in the business of always putting the customer first, and offering a fully integrated approach that is convenient, seamless, and reliable. "Most people are unaware of the complexity of the process," Mullen adds. "The ultimate compliment is when someone is coming out of the closing and says, 'This was a good experience. . . . Thank you for making it easy.'" ■

> Professionals Title Company is in the business of always putting the customer first.

PHOTO BY DOUG HENDERSON

Professional service and stress-free closings!
If those are your goals, always insist on Professionals Title to handle your closing requirements.

BOTH PHOTOS BY GENE BEDNAREK

Success in today's fast-paced business and academic worlds is based on a solid grounding in technology. "At Westwood Middle School we have a program that helps students understand technology, its development, and its uses," said James J. TenBieg, principal. "Laboratory experiences that include hands-on activities give students a chance to develop technological literacy, apply basic skills, learn problem-solving, and increase their self-awareness." Westwood is the largest middle school in the district, with approximately one thousand students.

GAINESVILLE — EVERY PATH *starts with* PASSION 175

BOTH PHOTOS BY ROD REILLY

The Harn Museum is not only a collection of treasures, it is a treasure in itself. Visitors like Jackie and Pamela Stanley know that in addition to its many collections, gardens, classroom spaces, and inviting café, it provides educational opportunities, films, lectures, gallery talks, and occasional performances. Located at the University of Florida Cultural Plaza on campus, the Harn is in the process of constructing a new wing to open in 2010. This new, twenty-thousand-square-foot space will be devoted to the exhibition, conservation, and study of the museum's Asian art collection. The museum also houses one of the largest African art collections in the Southeast.

GAINESVILLE — EVERY PATH *starts with* PASSION 177

PHOTO BY ROD REILLY

What better place to retire after an eventful day in Gainesville than the full-service luxury of the Gateway Grand? Its warm exterior is doubly matched by the cozy, yet elegant interior and friendly service designed to make every customer feel like royalty— and beloved pets are considered favored customers as well.

PHOTO BY DOUG HENDERSON

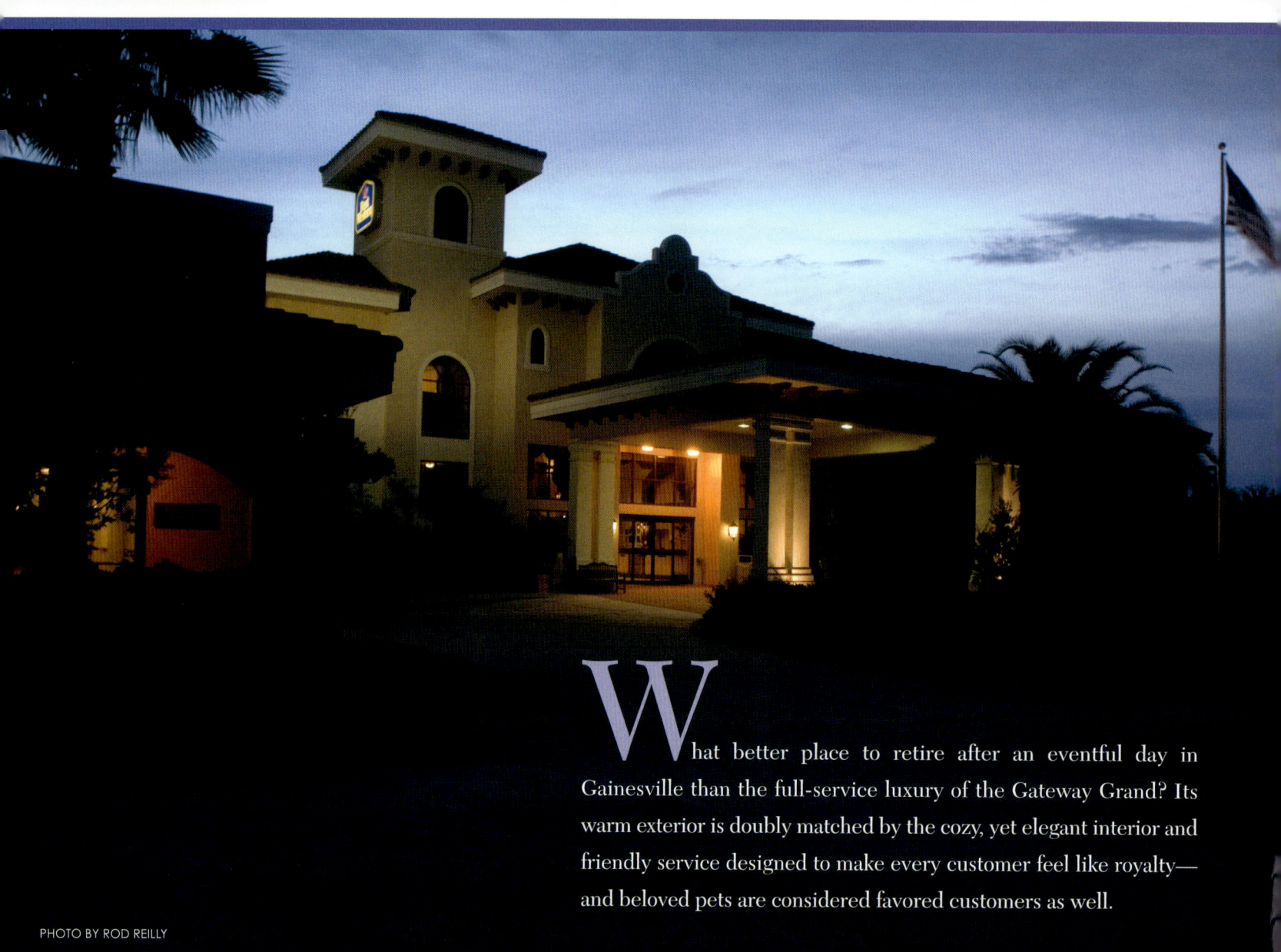

The Brytan sales team believes in one-on-one customer attention. Team member Joyce Dorval points out to a customer the many parks and green spaces.

178 GAINESVILLE — EVERY PATH *starts with* PASSION

BOTH PHOTOS BY GENE BEDNAREK

Since 1983, Thornebrook Village, a shopping center in Gainesville, has led the way in innovation: first, by becoming the first retail condominiums in Florida in which the shop owners also owned their buildings, and second, by bringing the concept of shopping in a park to life. Not only do Thornebrook's airy breezeways lead shoppers to one-of-a-kind purchasing opportunities, but mixed with surrounding green areas, they serve as the perfect tropical setting for an annual, two-day fine arts and crafts festival that is hailed as the finest small arts show in the southeastern United States. Artisans vie for the limited spaces to show their beautiful wares in this colorful display of crafts, characters, and even cockatoos sponsored by the Gainesville Fine Arts Association and the Thornebrook Merchants Association.

GAINESVILLE — EVERY PATH *starts with* PASSION

PHOTO BY DOUG HENDERSON

The dramatic lighting and the tension between Oliver and the menacing character Bill Sikes in *Oliver* exemplify just one more in a long line of outstanding productions by the Gainesville Community Playhouse. The theatre group gave its first performance in 1927, and like Oliver, audiences have been begging for "More" ever since. The first production was *The Pied Piper of Hamlin* for "children of all ages." It was a great success, and to satisfy the interest of the adult audience, the first performance by the adult members of the group opened on May 13, 1932. GCP is the oldest community theatre in Florida. Today they perform in the luxurious Vam York Theatre and produce a regular season of six plays a year, usually three musicals and three dramas or comedies.

The Gainesville Ballet Theatre certainly knows how to keep dance enthusiasts on their toes. Each holiday season, patrons young and old prepare themselves to be whisked away to the world of *The Little Match Girl*, courtesy of some of the area's most talented ballerinas, who tell the story of the enchanting child with the same prowess exhibited by the finest dance professionals in the world. The production, which has been a tradition in Gainesville since the late 1970s and is held annually at the Curtis M. Phillips Center for the Performing Arts, undoubtedly is one of the highlights of the year for Joni Messler, founder of the nonprofit regional company and owner and director of the Joni Messler Studio of Dance. Through her vision, hundreds of gifted and dedicated dancers have had the opportunity to study ballet, perform for audiences throughout Gainesville, and go on to thriving and artistically challenging careers.

BOTH PHOTOS BY DOUG HENDERSON

GAINESVILLE — EVERY PATH *starts with* PASSION   181

Office of University of Florida Research

University of Florida Office of Research: Teaching, Research, and Service

As one of the nation's most comprehensive institutions, the University of Florida is uniquely situated to pursue cutting-edge research and education in the twenty-first century. With twenty colleges and schools on its picturesque two-thousand-acre campus, faculty members in fields as diverse as medicine, law, and agriculture can literally walk across the street to collaborate.

The University of Florida is uniquely situated to pursue cutting-edge research and education in the twenty-first century.

"At the University of Florida, all the ingredients needed for top-notch interdisciplinary research are located on our one campus," says Win Phillips, the university's vice president for research.

UF's more than four thousand faculty members recognize the opportunities that interdisciplinary research offers and actively seek collaborations with colleagues outside their own fields. These faculty aggressively pursue external funding for their research, garnering a record $583 million in 2007.

Research also contributes to the quality of UF's educational experience, offering more than thirty-five thousand undergraduates and fifteen thousand graduate and professional students unparalleled opportunities for hands-on learning in the classroom, the laboratory, and the field.

UF is a national leader in transferring knowledge to the marketplace. The best-known product to come out of the university is Gatorade™, the world's leading sports drink, which has brought more than $150 million in royalties to the university since its creation in 1965. The royalties from Gatorade and numerous other products—including the Sentricon termite elimination technology and the Trusopt glaucoma treatment—have been rolled back into the research enterprise to foster the next generation of discoveries. ■

PHOTO BY GENE BEDNAREK

Win Phillips, vice president for research at the University of Florida, at the new Cancer & Genetics Research Building, part of a construction renaissance on campus that will result in more than six hundred thousand square feet of new research space by 2010.

182 GAINESVILLE — Every Path starts with Passion

A magnificent specimen of an American mastodon greets visitors to the Florida Museum of Natural History. Located in the Cultural Plaza on the University of Florida campus, the museum's collections provide a look at the state's natural history. From ancient fossils to water environments to Native Peoples, the museum's exhibits preserve and interpret various segments of the area's natural and cultural past. Exhibits also include a unique butterfly rainforest as well as gardens featuring native wildflowers and modern species of ancient plants.

PHOTO BY ROD REILLY

RTI/Biologics is one of the University of Florida's most successful technology transfer programs, earning the university millions for reinvestment into research and new medical facilities. RTI scientists invented the BioCleanse® Tissue Sterilization Process, clinically proven to eliminate donor-to-recipient disease transmission.

GAINESVILLE — EVERY PATH *starts with* PASSION

184 GAINESVILLE — Every Path *starts with* Passion

ALL PHOTOS BY DOM MARTINO

As one of the nation's most important natural resources, Paynes Prairie Preserve State Park has remained largely unchanged for centuries. A place of serene beauty and wonder, the twenty-one-thousand-acre preserve is home to hundreds of plant species as well as an impressive variety of wildlife. Visitors to the preserve can observe everything from alligators and wild horses to hawks and bald eagles. Other features of the preserve include hiking, biking, and horseback riding trails as well as canoeing or boating opportunities and fishing on Lake Wauberg.

Moving so fast the world is just a blur, longtime server Dixie Newsome makes sure her customers get their food while it's piping hot. For more than twenty years the Conestogas Restaurant in Alachua has been pleasing its clientele with great food served with a smile. The secret to all this deliciousness is that the restaurant hand trims all the sirloins, ribeyes, filet mignons, and New York strip steaks, and then grinds the hamburgers from the steak trimmings. Just one of Conestogas' sixteen-ounce Stogie burgers on a big toasted bun, and you'll be hooked for life.

PHOTO BY GENE BEDNAREK

186 GAINESVILLE — EVERY PATH *starts with* PASSION

(Left to right) Polly Crooks, office staff, with Jan and Anna van Rooyen, owners of Gainesville Violins, a local workshop that specializes in everything violin. In addition to restoration and sales of antique and modern versions, the shop custom makes violins for customers around the world. Born and raised in South Africa, the van Rooyens operated a violin shop there before arriving in America in 1997. Today, they travel the world in search of violins and continue to share their love of music through three shops in Florida.

PHOTO BY ROD REILLY

GAINESVILLE — EVERY PATH *starts with* PASSION 187

PHOTO BY GENE BEDNAREK

Stained glass represents the perfect blend of art and function. Masterpieces made using the medium are as beautiful as they are utilitarian, and no one in Gainesville is as skilled or as proficient in the craft as Mike and Mary McIntyre, proprietors of McIntyre Stained Glass Studio & Art Gallery. Their awe-inspiring and award-winning work can be seen in churches, restaurants, stores, offices, and homes throughout the city. Their work can be found in their own gallery as well, which also provides a home for the art of more than two dozen local artists who work in everything from watercolors and pastels to blown glass and turned wood. But the McIntyres do much more than simply showcase the work of their colleagues in their studio; they also strive to help novice artisans find their own creative vision. Throughout the year, the couple presents two-hour classes for people who wish to learn how to design their own stained-glass masterpieces.

PHOTO BY DOUG HENDERSON

T he action seems to comes alive in the home of Tommy Waters ever since Custom Home Entertainment installed a state-of-the art home theatre.

PHOTO BY DOUG HENDERSON

190 GAINESVILLE — Every Path *starts with* Passion

From its start as a seminary in 1853, the University of Florida has grown into the largest university in the state and one of the nation's premier educational institutions. Each year, the school counts some fifty thousand students among its enrollment, working toward degrees in sixteen colleges offering a variety of studies in the areas of agriculture, architecture, arts, business, education, health, and more. The school is also home to more than one hundred centers and institutes focused on research and is a model of success for taking discoveries to market.

Gainesville
Featured Companies

Alachua County Biotech Industry

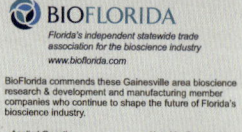

Applied Genetic Technologies Corporation
11801 Research Drive, Suite D
Alachua, Florida 32615
386.462.2204
www.agtc.com

BioFlorida Inc.
222 Lakeview Avenue, Fourth Floor
West Palm Beach, Florida 33401
561.653.3839
www.bioflorida.com

NovaMin Technology Inc.
13859 Progress Boulevard, #600
Alachua, Florida 32615
386.418.1551
www.novamin.com

RTI/Biologics
11621 Research Circle
Alachua, Florida 32615
386.418.8888
www.rtix.com

University of Florida Sid Martin Biotechnology Incubator
12085 Research Drive
Alachua, Florida 32615
386.462.0880
www.biotech.ufl.org

Biotechnology (58–60)
One of the nation's fastest-growing life-science industry clusters is in the Gainesville area, where more than forty-five biotechnology, medical device manufacturing, and medical research companies, employing tens of thousands of people, are working to help others lead healthier lives.

Alarion Bank
4373 Newberry Road
Gainesville, Florida 32607
352.224.1900
www.alarionbank.com

Financial Services—Bank (72–73)
Alarion Bank was formed in 2005 and is now one of the fastest-growing community banks in Florida—with three branches in Alachua County, three in Marion County, and more than $200 million in assets. The bank is owned by local investors, managed by local personnel, and staffed by local employees, all serving the Gainesville area with the best customer service and the latest in cutting-edge technology.

Barry Rutenberg Homes
P.O. Box 358080
Gainesville, Florida 32635
352.373.8466

Home Builder (42)
Designing and constructing custom and modifiable inventory homes in Alachua County since 1973, Barry Rutenberg Homes has also built a reputation for quality service. An award-winning builder, Rutenberg and his highly skilled staff determine their success via client satisfaction, demonstrated by repeat customers, customer referral, and a word-of-mouth positive reputation for listening and attending to homeowners' needs.

192 GAINESVILLE — EVERY PATH *starts with* PASSION

Best Western Gateway Grand
4200 NW 97th Boulevard
Gainesville, Florida 32606
352.331.3336
www.gatewaygrand.com

Lodging—Hotel (44–47)
Located on rolling hills dotted with giant Southern oaks, the Best Western Gateway Grand offers the feel of a country retreat that is conveniently located near the nightlife of Gainesville. This nonsmoking, pet-friendly hotel offers the best of amenities and hospitable service in its guest rooms, specialty suites, ballrooms, and conference and business centers.

Bosshardt Realty Services Inc.
5542 NW 43rd Street
Gainesville, Florida 32653
352.371.6100
www.bosshardtrealty.com

Real Estate Agency (34–39)
Bosshardt Realty Services Inc. is an independent, locally owned and operated business. It combines a close personal relationship with employees, associates, and the people the company serves with the qualities of a leading-edge, professional company. The biggest real estate company in Gainesville, Bosshardt Realty has its own human resources, IT, and marketing departments, plus the best in-house training program in the area.

Brame Architects
606 NE 1st Street
Gainesville, Florida 32601
352.372.0425
www.bramearchitects.com

Architectural Firm (102–103)
Brame Architects, in business since 1911, offers a comprehensive scope of services for clients in the public and private sectors. Its jobs range from large to small—from governmental administrative and office buildings, to churches and educational facilities at all grade levels, to single-family and multifamily residential properties. The firm also works on historic preservation projects.

Brice Development Inc.
5995 SW 75th Street
Gainesville, Florida 32608
352.379.5777
www.brytan.com

Real Estate—Developer (25–27)
Promising future residents the unexpected in the everyday, Brice Development Group has planned Brytan, a modern mixed-use neighborhood with the convenience and warmth of a small town. With home lots and commercial space now available, Brytan offers a variety of housing options, a town center, dining, shopping, and the best of technology in a development that showcases the quality lifestyle of New Urbanism.

Charles Perry Construction
8200 NW 15th Place
Gainesville, Florida 32606
352.331.4088
www.perryconstruction.com

Contractor—General (162–163)
From offices to educational facilities to hospitals to manufacturing plants, Charles Perry Construction has completed projects of every size and scope in the full range of industries. Its success is derived from a solid reputation for completing work that exceeds client expectations.

Clariant Life Science Molecules (FL) Inc.
P.O. Box 1466
Gainesville, Florida 32602
352.376.8246
www.clariant.com

Manufacturing Company—Chemicals (30–31)
Clariant is a global leader in the field of specialty chemicals. The products and services of the Gainesville site are based on the development and manufacture of innovative specialty chemicals. These products and services play a decisive role in their customers' manufacturing processes and upgrade their finished products. Clariant is a world-class employer and responsible corporate citizen that sponsors—among other charities—the annual Alachua County Science Teacher of the Year award.

Compass Bank
2814 SW 34th Street
Gainesville, Florida 32614
352.367.5064
www.compassbank.com

Financial Services—Bank (62)
A corporate citizen with the community's best interest in mind, Compass Bank focuses on individual, commercial, industrial, and private banking. With a resolve to make every customer's experience better at every turn, this bank continually meets its goal to make a positive difference for Gainesville's citizens and businesses.

GAINESVILLE — EVERY PATH *starts with* PASSION 193

Crime Prevention Security Systems and Custom Home Entertainment
4701 SW 34th Street
Gainesville, Florida 32608
352.332.6100
www.CPSS.net

Security Systems and Home Entertainment (66–69)
As the leading low-voltage, full-technology integrator in the area, Crime Prevention Security Systems and its newest division, Custom Home Entertainment, provide design, installation, service, and monitoring of security and fire alarm systems, as well as home/office networking, distributed audio, and home theater.

ERA Trend Realty
4141 NW 37th Place
Gainesville, Florida 32606
352.225.4700
www.eratrend.com

Real Estate—Commercial and Residential (172–173)
ERA Trend Realty has been operating in the Gainesville market since 1974. The firm has an ever-expanding sales force that constantly undergoes in-house training to concentrate on customers' needs and deliver the best service possible. The firm and its associates focus their support on the University of Florida's Cultural Plaza, the crown jewel of the Gainesville community.

Exactech Inc.
2320 NW 66th Court
Gainesville, Florida 32653
352.377.1140
www.exac.com

Manufacturing Company—Artificial Joints (108–109)
Exactech is a publicly held medical device company that develops, manufactures, and markets artificial implants and biologic materials for joint restoration surgery. Over the past twenty years, the company has enjoyed rapid growth with approximately three hundred employees, more than fifty independent sales agencies across the United States, and distribution in over thirty countries. Exactech was recognized by *The Wall Street Journal* in 2007 as a Top Small Workplace.

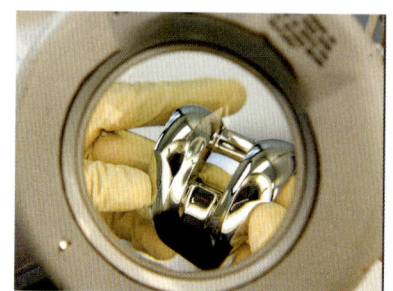

Fletcher Mortgage Company
106 SW 140th Terrace, Suite 3
Newberry, Florida 32669
352.331.5152
www.fletchermortgage.net

Financial Services—Mortgage Company (112–115)
Fletcher Mortgage Company is a full-service brokerage that operates on the belief in going the distance for clients. Owned and operated by a fourth-generation Gainesville, Floridian, Fletcher Mortgage has developed strong relationships with area financial institutions, enhancing the company's ability to listen to clients and find the best fit in financing for residential or commercial needs. Fletcher Mortgage is part of a group of family-owned real estate companies that collectively make buying, selling, developing, and financing real estate as easy as one-stop shopping.

Florida Citizens Bank
3919 W. Newberry Road
Gainesville, Florida 32607
352.332.4727
www.floridacitizensbank.com

Financial Services—Bank (80–83)
Florida Citizens Bank is the "7 to 7 Community Bank," offering a complete line of personal and commercial banking products and services. The bank's unique programs for businesses include Customer Care, a daily e-mailed spreadsheet of account activity; Remote Deposit Capture, allowing business owners to send deposits electronically; and corporate credit cards with instant credit increases and a monthly breakdown of expenditures categorized for tax purposes.

FloridaWorks
300 University Avenue, Suite 100
Gainesville, Florida 32601
352.334.7100
www.floridaworksonline.com

Nonprofit—Workforce Development (106)
FloridaWorks is a business-oriented organization dedicated to growing businesses and jobs through a skilled workforce. FloridaWorks. Everybody works.

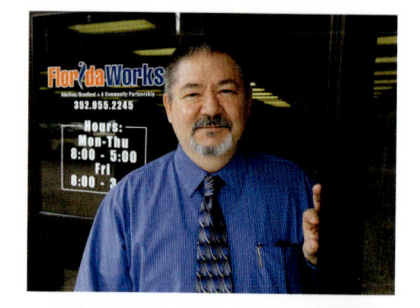

Gainesville Area Chamber of Commerce
300 E. University Avenue, Suite 100
Gainesville, Florida 32601
352.334.7100
www.gainesvillechamber.com

Chamber of Commerce (76–77)
As an advocate for business, the Gainesville Area Chamber of Commerce fosters a healthy business climate through involvement in activities that make doing business easier. Its member services provide networking and educational opportunities, and its Council for Economic Outreach is focused on economic development. The chamber also serves as an active voice in policy issues at the state and local levels.

Gainesville Harley-Davidson & Buell
4125 NW 97th Boulevard
Gainesville, Florida 32606
352.331.6363
www.gainesvilleharley.com

Retail—Motorcycle Dealership (86–87)
Gainesville Harley-Davidson & Buell is a family-owned company and the only Harley dealership in Gainesville. It opened in 1993 in a small space and today occupies more than twenty-five thousand square feet. Among approximately 650 Harley-Davidson dealers in the United States, Gainesville Harley-Davidson & Buell has earned nine awards, based largely on their customer service. Excellent products and outstanding customer service continue to drive Gainesville Harley-Davidson & Buell into the future.

Gainesville Health & Fitness Centers
4820 W. Newberry Road
Gainesville, Florida 32607
352.377.4955
www.ghfc.com

Health Club (166–168)
The Gainesville Health & Fitness Center has three facilities totaling 105,000 square feet. The company is the only fitness center in Gainesville to receive the honor of Business of the Year by the Gainesville Area Chamber of Commerce and Entrepreneur of the Year by the University of Florida.

Haven Hospice
4200 NW 90th Boulevard
Gainesville, Florida 32606
800.727.1889
www.havenhospice.org

Nonprofit—Hospice (156)
Established in 1979 and licensed by the state since 1980, Haven Hospice serves sixteen counties in North Florida, providing comprehensive, compassionate care for patients with life-limiting illnesses, according to each person's needs, beliefs, or wishes.

Infinite Energy
7001 SW 24th Avenue
Gainesville, Florida 32607
352.331.1654
www.infiniteenergy.com

Marketing Firm—Energy Products (132–133)
Infinite Energy Inc., headquartered in Gainesville, markets wholesale and retail energy products. In Florida, industrial companies, institutions, governments, and large and small commercial businesses purchase natural gas from Infinite. In Georgia, New York, and New Jersey, Infinite also serves residential customers.

James Moore & Co., P.L.
5931 NW 1st Place
Gainesville, Florida 32607
352.378.1331
www.jmco.com

CPA Firm (136–137)
James Moore & Co., P.L. (JM&Co.), is one of the largest accounting firms in Florida. With offices in Gainesville, Tallahassee, and Daytona Beach, the firm offers an array of tax, audit, accounting, and information systems consulting services to clients throughout Florida. JM&Co. employs more than one hundred professionals—all dedicated to providing clients with exceptional service and supporting the surrounding community.

Keith Watson Productions
2425 NW 71st Place
Gainesville, Florida 32653
352.264.8812
www.KeithWatsonProductions.com

Event Productions (124–125)
Keith Watson Productions is a special-events company servicing corporate and private clients in North Central Florida, metropolitan New York, and the tri-state area. The company provides complete special-event solutions, from design to implementation.

M.M. Parrish Construction Company
3455 SW 42nd Avenue
Gainesville, Florida 32608
352.378.1571
www.mmpcc.com

Contractor—General (140–142)
M.M. Parrish Construction Company is made up of construction managers, design builders, and general contractors. Beginning in the early 1940s and incorporated in 1968, it is a company of the highest integrity, providing outstanding service to clients and rewarding opportunities to employees, and operating as a good corporate citizen throughout the Gainesville area.

Marriott Residence Inn
4001 SW 13th Street
Gainesville, Florida 32608
352.371.2101
www.marriott.com/hotels/travel/gnvfl-residence-inn-gainesville

Lodging—Hotel (158–159)
With a passion for making every guest feel welcome, Marriott Residence Inn offers all the comforts of home. The hotel offers eighty suites on two floors, complimentary breakfast, business services, and much more.

Meridian Behavioral Healthcare Inc.
4300 SW 13th Street
Gainesville, Florida 32608
352.374.5600
www.mbhci.org

Nonprofit—Rehabilitation Center (128)
For thirty-five years, Meridian Behavioral Healthcare Inc., headquartered in Gainesville, has extended help and hope to thousands of people who experience addiction, mental illnesses, and other social challenges. With inpatient and outpatient services for children and adults, the nonprofit center strives to give its patients the skills and coping strategies that enable them to become productive community members.

North Florida Regional Medical Center
6500 Newberry Road
Gainesville, Florida 32605
352.333.4000
www.nfrmc.com

Health Care—Medical Center (120–121)
Founded by a group of physicians in 1972, North Florida Regional Medical Center (NFRMC) has over four hundred physicians on staff representing forty different specialties. NFRMC is among an elite few nonteaching hospitals to be recognized eight times as one of the nation's 100 Top Hospitals. The campus on Newberry Road is a familiar landmark and a symbol of NFRMC's permanent commitment to the community.

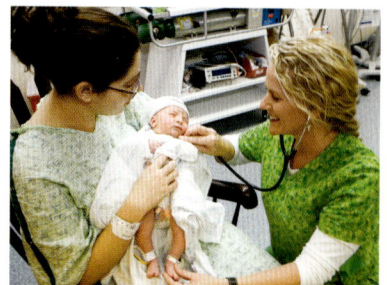

Office of University of Florida Research
P.O. Box 115500
University of Florida
Gainesville, Florida 32611
352.392.1582
www.research.ufl.edu

School—University Research Center (182)
The University of Florida is a major, public, comprehensive, land-grant research university. It is the state's oldest, largest, and most comprehensive university. The success of Gatorade is well known, but it is just one of many UF products that have benefited countless people. Other important research products include Trusopt, a leading treatment for glaucoma, and the Sentricon Termite Elimination System.

PPI Construction Management
8200 NW 15th Place, Suite B
Gainesville, Florida 32606
352.331.1141
www.ppicm.com

Construction Management (144–145)
With headquarters in Gainesville, and offices in Orlando and Flagler Beach, PPI Construction Management has grown to be a premiere construction management firm in Florida. The company provides services to educational, health-care, institutional, criminal justice, and government markets throughout Florida and the United States.

Professionals Title Company
4141 NW 37th Place
Gainesville, Florida 32606
352.225.4600
www.professionalstitlecompany.com

Real Estate—Title Company (174)
Professionals Title Company provides residential and commercial title insurance and real estate closing services. The company is a member of the Title Resource Group, a national leader in the title and settlement industry.

Santa Fe Community College
3000 NW 83rd Street
Gainesville, Florida 32606
352.395.5000
www.sfcc.edu

School—College (90-93)
Santa Fe Community College has a mission of adding value to the lives of its students and enriching the community. With more than seventeen thousand students, the college offers degrees and certificates leading to university transfer or more than sixty different careers. It also provides many noncredit opportunities through Community Education, College for Kids, and PrimeTime Institute for seniors.

SantaFe HealthCare Inc./ AvMed Health Plans
4300 NW 89th Boulevard
Gainesville, Florida 32606
352.372.8400

Health Care—Services (152–154)
SantaFe HealthCare, Inc., a $1 billion community-based holding company headquartered in Gainesville, operates facilities with a focus on maintaining and supporting optimal health and hearty lifestyles. From health incentive and insurance programs offered by AvMed Health Plans, to its upscale retirement communities (North Florida Retirement Village and Bayview Gardens), to caring hospice and palliative care (Haven Hospice), SantaFe HealthCare consistently makes its mark as a national leader in providing quality services for every stage of life.

Shands HealthCare
1600 SW Archer Road
Gainesville, Florida 32608
352.265.0111
www.shands.org

Health Care—Hospital System (96–97)
Shands HealthCare is a private, not-for-profit health-care system affiliated with the University of Florida. Patients benefit from the collective resources of Shands HealthCare's eight not-for-profit hospitals and home health services and the network of more than eighty affiliated UF primary care and specialty practices throughout North Central and Northeast Florida.

Tioga Realty
105 SW 128th Street, Suite 200
Gainesville, Florida 32669
352.333.3009
www.tiogarealty.com

Real Estate—Commercial and Residential (148–149)
Tioga Realty is a full-service real estate agency whose associates have the expertise, experience, and compassion to ensure client success. Whether a client is buying a first home, building a custom home, locating a business, or looking for land to develop, Tioga Realty can help with any real estate transaction.

Tioga Town Center
105 SW 128th Street, Suite 200
Tioga, Florida 32669
352.331.4000
www.tiogatowncenter.com

Real Estate—Developer (18–21)
Tioga Town Center is the commercial and retail development at the heart of the Town of Tioga. Featuring residential, retail, commercial, and office space, the mixed-use center provides members of the community with a convenient live-work-play atmosphere that reflects design principles of the past and building principles of the future.

Town of Tioga
13151 Newberry Road
Gainesville, Florida 32669
352.331.6220
www.townoftioga.com

Real Estate—Developer (54–55)
The Town of Tioga is the brainchild of developers Miguel and Luis Diaz. Located five minutes west of I-75, the community offers a traditional family-first lifestyle, with charming homes featuring inviting front porches and outstanding community amenities like pedestrian-friendly streets, a town promenade, Tioga Town Center, and much more. It is the recipient of the 1998 ENVY Award from the Florida Association of Realtors and the Gold Award for Best Smart Growth Community in the nation from the National Association of Home Builders.

UF Orthopaedic and Sports Medicine Institute
3450 Hull Road
Gainesville, Florida 32611
352.273.7001
www.ortho.ufl.edu

Health-Care Physicians Group (52)
The UF Orthopaedic and Sports Medicine Institute is focused on collaborative science and treatment for musculoskeletal disorders. OSMI treats more than one hundred thousand patients a year from all states and several foreign countries in a spacious and technologically advanced environment.

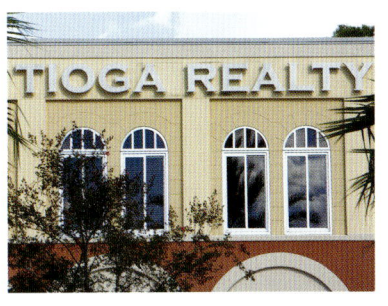

Thank you for your support!

Gainesville Editorial Team

Kimberly Fox DeMeza, Writer, Roswell, Georgia. Combining business insight with creative flair, DeMeza writes to engage the audience as well as communicate the nuances of the subject matter. Officially beginning her career in public relations in 1980 with a degree in journalism, and following in 1990 with a master's in health management, writing has always been central to her professional experience. From speechwriting to corporate brochures to business magazine feature writing, DeMeza enjoys the process of crafting the message. Delving into the topic is simply one of the benefits, as she believes every writing opportunity is an opportunity to continue to learn.

Rena Distasio, Writer, Tijeras, New Mexico. Freelance writer Rena Distasio contributes articles and reviews on a variety of subjects to regional and national publications. She also edits two magazines focused on life in the Four Corners region. In her spare time she and her husband and their dog enjoy the great outdoors from their home in the mountains east of Albuquerque.

Grace Hawthorne, Writer, Atlanta, Georgia. Starting as a reporter, she has written everything from advertising for septic tanks to the libretto for an opera. While in New York, she worked for Time-Life Books and wrote for *Sesame Street*. As a performer, she has appeared at the Carter Presidential Center, Callanwolde Fine Arts Center, and at various corporate functions. Her latest project is a two-woman show called *Pushy Broads and Proper Southern Ladies*.

Amy Meadows, Writer, Canton, Georgia. Meadows is an accomplished feature writer who has been published in a wide variety of local, regional, and national consumer and trade publications since launching her freelance writing career in 2000. She also specializes in producing corporate marketing literature for companies large and small and holds a master of arts degree in professional writing from Kennesaw State University.

Regina Roths, Writer, Andover, Kansas. Roths has written extensively about business since launching her journalism career in the early 1990s. Her prose can be found in corporate coffee-table books nationwide as well as on regionally produced Web sites, and in print and online magazines, newspapers, and publications. Her love of industry, history, and research gives her a keen insight into writing and communicating a message.

Gail Snyder, Writer, Woodstock, Georgia. Snyder is a writer and editor with twenty years of experience in corporate communications and publishing. She has edited or written articles focusing on corporate management strategies, published articles in a number of trade magazines and journals, and edited both fiction and nonfiction books. Gail enjoys explaining material to an audience in a way that reveals how any subject can be interesting. She earned her bachelor's degree in journalism from Georgia State University, where she went on to complete her master's in communications. Currently she works as a freelance and contract writer and editor.

Gene Bednarek, Photographer, Atlantic Beach, Florida. With over twenty years of experience in creating work for reproduction, Bednarek has worked with hundreds of national and international publications producing portraits and illustrations for corporate and editorial use. His work has been exhibited widely throughout the United States, including New York City, and his photos reside in many corporate, public, and private collections. His business, Southlight Publishing, services clients in the travel, hospitality, and magazine fields. When not photographing for work or pleasure, Bednarek enjoys fishing and camping with his family, wife Kim and sons Jackson and Clayton.

Douglas Henderson, Photographer, Tulsa, Oklahoma. Doug is a commercial photographer and graphic designer. As a professional photographer, his work has appeared in *The New York Times*, *Newsweek*, *Newsweek Japan*, the *National Enquirer*, and others. He has worked in the United States, Mexico, South Africa, Ghana, and Côte D'Ivoire. He is the author of several textbooks on digital photography and Adobe Photoshop. See more of his work online at www.douglashenderson.com.

Scott Indermaur, Photographer, East Greenwich, Rhode Island. Indermaur's assignments have taken him from the smallest rural communities to the world's most urban environments. His gift lies in discovering the familiar in the exotic and the remarkable in the ordinary. Whether he's capturing a fleeting moment in history or cutting to the essence of a portrait, Scott tells the story in a language everyone understands. When not photographing, Scott—who along with his wife, daughter, and son are all Tae Kwon Do black belts—also enjoys wonderful food and wine, meeting new people, traveling, music, and sailing. You can view his images and contact him at www.siphotography.com.

Rod Reilly, Photographer, Atlanta, Georgia. Since 1979 Reilly has used his training at Carnegie Mellon School of Design and Rochester Institute of Technology to create compelling environmental portraits on location of people as they live and work. His clients include Home Depot, Coca-Cola USA, United Parcel Service, Cox Communications, and McGraw-Hill. Starting his career as a staff shooter for Georgia Pacific, Rod has owned his own studio, Reilly Arts & Letters, for the last twelve years, and travels often on assignment. He is a member of ASMP and the father of three.

Alan S. Weiner, Photographer, Portland, Oregon. Weiner travels extensively both in the United States and abroad. Over the last twenty-three years his work has appeared regularly in *The New York Times*. In addition, his pictures have been published in *USA Today* and in *Time*, *Newsweek*, *Life*, and *People* magazines. He has shot corporate work for IBM, Pepsi, UPS, and other companies large and small. He is also the cofounder of the Wedding Bureau (www.weddingbureau.com). Alan has worked in every region of the country for Riverbend Books. His strengths are in photojournalism.

About the Publisher

GAINESVILLE — EVERY PATH *starts with* PASSION was published by Bookhouse Group, Inc., under its imprint of Riverbend Books. What many people don't realize is that in addition to picture books on American communities, we also develop and publish institutional histories, commemorative books of all types, contemporary books, and others for clients across the country.

Bookhouse has developed various types of books for prep schools from Utah to Florida, colleges and universities, country clubs, a phone company in Vermont, a church in Atlanta, hospitals, banks, and many other entities. We've also published a catalog for an art collection for a gallery in Texas, a picture book for a worldwide Christian ministry, and a book on a priceless collection of art and antiques for the Atlanta History Center.

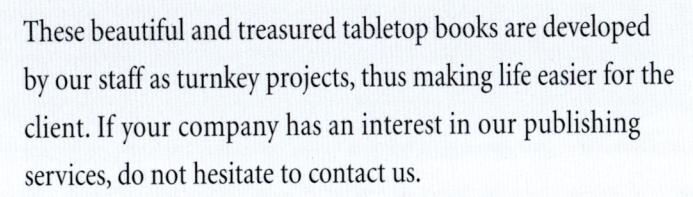

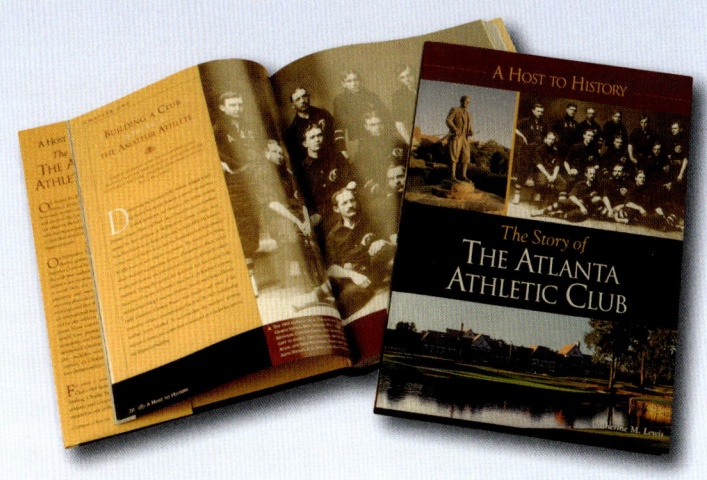

These beautiful and treasured tabletop books are developed by our staff as turnkey projects, thus making life easier for the client. If your company has an interest in our publishing services, do not hesitate to contact us.

Founded in 1989, Bookhouse Group is headquartered in a renovated 1920s tobacco warehouse in downtown Atlanta. If you're ever in town, we'd be delighted if you looked us up. Thank you for making possible the publication of **GAINESVILLE — EVERY PATH *starts with* PASSION**.

BOOKHOUSE® GROUP, INC.

Banks ❖ Prep Schools ❖ Hospitals
❖ Insurance Companies ❖ Art Galleries
❖ Museums ❖ Utilities ❖ Country Clubs
❖ Colleges ❖ Churches
❖ Military Academies ❖ Associations

PHOTO BY GENE BEDNAREK

When Ponce De Leon discovered the crystal springs of Florida, he thought he had found the fountain of youth. In a way, he may have been right. Gainesville has been voted Number One of the 50 Best Places to Work and Play by *National Geographic Adventure* magazine, and AARP lists it as one of the 15 Best Places to Reinvent Your Life. Gainesville citizens have carefully preserved its historic buildings and the beauty of its natural surroundings. The city's lush landscapes and urban "forest" make Gainesville one of the most attractive cities in Florida. It is also home to Florida's largest and oldest university, and is one of the state's centers of education, medicine, cultural events, and athletics. Put all that together and you have the recipe for a long, happy, healthy life . . . in short, the fountain of youth.

200 GAINESVILLE — EVERY PATH *starts with* PASSION